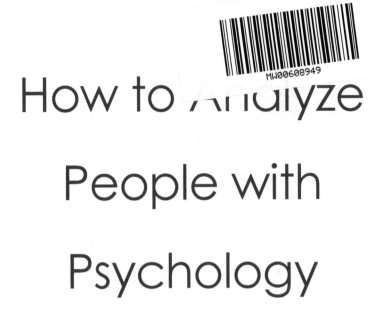

How to Analyze People with Psychology

The Ultimate Guide to Speed-Reading People through Body Language Analysis and Behavioral Psychology

Emotional Pathway

Table of Contents

Download the Audio Book Version of This Book for FREE

If you love listening to audiobooks on-the-go, I have great news for you. You can download the audiobook version of this book for FREE just by signing up for a FREE 30-day Audible trial! See below for more details!

Audible Trial Benefits

As an audible customer, you will receive the below benefits with your 30-day free trial:

- FREE audible book copy of this book

- After the trial, you will get one credit each month to use on any audiobook

- Your credits automatically roll over to the next month if you don't use them

- Choose from Audible's 200,000 + titles

- Listen anywhere with the Audible app across multiple devices

- Make easy, no-hassle exchanges of any audiobook you don't love

- Keep your audiobooks forever, even if you cancel your membership

- And much more

Click the links below to get started!

For the Audible US

For the Audible UK

For Audible FR

For Audible DE

Introduction

First off, I would like to thank you for purchasing *How to Analyze People with Psychology*. I hope you have as much fun using the information within these pages as I did writing it.

Most people know about the concept of body language and may understand it to a certain extent, but rarely do people know how to read it. It's called body language for a reason and is indeed a language. Just like different spoken languages are made up of words put together to form sentences, body language puts together mannerisms to create confidential information.

In this book, we will cover everything you need to know to understand body language. First off, we will look at the history of body language and how the ancient people used it. While it may be hard to believe, it has been understood for that long.

Then we will look at what you should look out for when you first meet a person. First impressions are essential, and the way a person acts when they first meet, you can tell you a lot about them.

Then we will look at manipulative personalities. Next to first impressions, this is an important thing to understand right off so that you don't end up getting trapped by the manipulative person. Manipulative people try to hide their actions, so it takes a little more work to spot these signals.

Next up, we will look at how the brain controls a person's body language. Why is our body let us down and say one thing when, verbally, we are telling another? It all has to do with the brain.

Then we will dive into the depth of body language. We will travel from top to bottom and discuss every part of the body and its movements and what they mean. There is a lot, so make sure you are prepared.

In the next chapter, we will look at breathing. While this may not seem important, the breath can let you in on a lot about another person. Just take a moment to think about how differently you breathe when you are relaxed, happy, scared, and angry.

Then we will pick the face apart in the next chapter. We will look at what is called micro-expressions and what they all mean. The face tends to hold much information, so it's essential to be aware of a person's face does as they are talking and listening.

Lastly, we will look at how to spot a liar. Nobody likes to be lied to, so this information will help you to know if somebody is doing just that. You will need to use this information wisely, however. It wouldn't look good if you jumped down somebody's throat for lying when you aren't sure they are.

I also want to take some time to go over some ground rules. You must read this book from start to finish. Don't try to learn everything the first time you read through the book. Simply read through and try to pick up what you can. After that, go through it again and take some notes. Then you can start trying to learn body language.

Once you think you are ready to start reading body language, practice with movies, magazines, and TV. When you are waiting to check out at the grocery store, look through the magazine, and see if you can figure out what a person feels. This is also a great game to play when you are watching talk shows. See how guests act and respond to the questions the host asks and see if they are genuine or trying to hide something.

Then you can move to look at those around you. When you know somebody is getting ready to ask you for something, watch how they act. This will be different for everybody, but it is something helpful to know because you will be able to spot when they want something before they ask.

Before you get started analyzing people, those whom you work with, family, and friends, there is something that you have to do before you start reading them. You must clear your head of prejudice. Prejudices can be something like assuming big people are lazy or judging somebody differently because you don't think they are pretty.

These things should not influence your reading of their body language. This gives you a false understanding, and you can end up treating them in the wrong way for no reason.

The problem is that these prejudices have been programmed into you since a young age. The things people believe are deceiving. It creates a warped view of reality. Here are some easy ways to clear these thoughts out of your mind so that you can read body language accurately.

- Take a little time. When you first meet a person, make sure you let yourself get to know them. You can't start judging their body language until you know them a bit, and you definitely can't interpret their body language if you are already assuming things based on the way they look. Let yourself take some time to get to know them before you start to understand something.

- Be sincere. Maybe you have already been given a negative view of a person. The truth is, you probably only have one side of the story. When you are an outside person and have heard things about somebody from only one person, especially when they are negative things, you can't judge their body language without finding out the truth. Nicely ask them about these negative things you have heard.

- Always try to find clarity. There are still going to be people who will try to skew your views about people for their benefit. You have to keep this from happening. You should try to reach your conclusions about people and gain clarity before you assume anything.

- Everybody is their person. Every single person in the world has the right to be whomever they want to be. They are all different, so you must accept that. You can't read a person thinking that they are like you because this will not give you an accurate reading. Accept the truth that people are different so that you can accurately interpret their body language.

8

You have to create some form of flexibility when you begin reading body language. You can't be rigid when there are so many different people in the world.

When you start to read people, the first thing you should look at is the full movement. Look at the way they are sitting or standing and how close they are to you. Do they want to be there? Do they lean towards you? Focus on these big things first. Then begin looking at the smaller movements; their hands, eyes, feet, and breathing.

What the significant movements try to hide, their smaller changes will tell you. Once you get used to reading body language, you can do so in whatever fashion works best for you.

After you have practiced reading body language and have cleared out prejudices, see how well you can figure out a person's tone of voice. See if you can tell how a person feels based solely on their mood. The sound is likely the most challenging part of the body language because there are similarities between emotions.

If you are unsure, go with your gut. Clear thoughts from your mind and your stomach will help you pick up on what you have learned and guide you. If you're not quite sure what their arms fold means, go with your gut. Intuitively, what do you believe it means? Your heart is hardly ever wrong.

Before we get into the good stuff, there is one last thing that I want to cover. These rules will help to ensure that you interpret body language correctly.

- Contextual – Gestures can easily be confused when interpreting body language. For example, if you are outside during the winter talking to a friend and sitting with their legs and arms crossed, thinking that they are defensive probably wouldn't be accurate. It is much more likely that they are cold. If they were in a different situation, it could be something different. A person who scratches their neck could mean indecision or uncertainty, but it could also mean that they need a shower. When two men shake hands, if one has a gentle handshake, it might show that they are weak, but he could also have arthritis. A woman in a short skirt is likely going to sit with her legs crossed, so you can't assume that she is defensive. It is so essential that you pay attention to the whole set before you judge body language.

- Cultural – Some body language is learned from the environment. This means that something healthy for one culture might not be the same as another. The most significant differences you may find between cultures are insult gestures, eye contact, touch frequency, and personal space. Spaniards and Italians like to kiss cheeks instead of shaking hands. A yes nod in Bulgaria means no. A surprise expression in Japan looks more like fear to Americans. The Japanese often nod and smile as they talk, so it doesn't necessarily mean that they agree with you. Men hold hands to show mutual respect in Saudi Arabia. For Americans, thumbs up mean okay. In Greece, it means "Up yours."

- Clusters – This is likely the most important thing to remember because it will help you with the first two. Every language comes with its own words that create sentences, and that's how body language works. Every gesture is simply a word. To understand what it means, you must look at their entire body, because that creates the sentence. Everybody has the tricks they have picked up over the years, so a single gesture isn't going to tell you much. For example, if a woman is playing with her hair, it might merely be a tick, but if crossed arms and legs accompany this action, it could show nervousness.

- Congruent – Congruence means that you see if the things they say and their body language match up. If a person has their legs and arms crossed and they seem upset, and you ask them, "Are you okay?" and they answer with "I'm fine," they are likely hiding something. This doesn't just live with words and gestures. It also includes their tone of voice. For example, saying, "I'm fine" with an angry tone lets you know that they aren't. Body language needs to be taken with a grain of salt. It isn't exact. Humans are an unpredictable bunch, so sometimes things did line up. Life is very variable, and the same is right for body language. Some people are fantastic at keeping eye contact when they aren't truthful, but others can't. Having some type of relationship with a person before you start analyzing them will help you out immensely.

I think that's enough for introductions. Let's get into the information that you came here for.

History of Body Language and Analysis

First off, I want to ask you a question, is body language we are born with or something we learn?

I don't expect you to answer because this question is pretty hard to answer because of two things.

First, body language is something that is evolved with time to match the social needs of humans. Some scientists and anthropologists study which gestures have developed and why we need them.

Secondly, within communication, body language can be divided into several different groups. There are some reactions and gestures that we are born with, and they are universal signals around the world. Others learn through observation and become refined with use and age.

So, the answer to the question is, it depends. For example, you weren't taught to scowl when you are angry. This was a programmed response in your brain of how to act when you feel mad. On the other hand, you have learned with time that standing up straight and smiling will project a positive image.

There is another question that some people like to ask, and that is, "Since we have words, do we need body language? Aren't we able to communicate without it?" The truth is that the use of speech is still a relatively new thing to human communication. Before we learned verbal communication, our communication skills were a lot like that of other animals, made up of non-verbal cues.

As you have probably heard, "old habits die hard," so that means body language still plays a massive part in our communication process, whether you want it to or not.

This can easily be seen when a person is speaking on the phone. While the person on the other end of the line can't see you, you probably still move around, wave your hands, and make facial expressions to stress your point. While it could seem primitive, during the time before we understood language, waving and grunting was enough to help us drive home a point.

You can't have real communication face to face without some type of body language. Verbal and nonverbal communications are two sides of the same coin. View body language as the "spice" that comes along with the main dish. You can say "I'm fine" in several ways with different facial expressions and tones, and every time it is going to affect the message.

Body language is non-verbal communication where physical actions are used to express a person's feelings. These actions include eye movement, touch, and space, gestures, posture, and facial expressions. Body language is present in humans as well as animals.

The Importance of Body Language

Body language is an essential part of the communication process that few have studied. It makes up most of our communication and tends to be more accurate than the things we say.

Everybody has heard that actions speak louder than words, and this is so true because there are many things that we communicate without ever saying a word. A simple shrug can tell a person, "I'm not sure." Raising your eyebrows can mean, "Did I hear that right?" Turning your palms face up and shrugging your shoulders could say, "I'm not sure what I should do." A simple point to the nose means, "That's right."

The body reinforces the things that we say. A person could say, "I'm not sure," or they could also turn the hands up, raise their eyebrows, frown a bit, and poke out their bottom lip. This will make a person laugh and relieve a bit of pressure if the situation is tense.

Why should a person take the time to learn the imprecise meanings of body language? Technically, the unconscious mind is already an expert at it, and the unconscious mind is more potent than that of the conscious mind. Why should we use our time and hard work to take this from our unconscious mind and move into the conscious mind, make this confusing, struggling with understanding it, before simply pushing it back into the unconscious mind after we stop focusing on it with the conscious mind?

I'm glad you asked.

This needs to be done because it gives us the chance to develop the skill of reading another person and control your body language. This means that you can communicate with intent instead of leaving things to chance.

For example, when we first meet a person, the unconscious mind begins to develop answers to questions that we have learned are essential. Are they going to hurt me? Are they bigger than me? Could they be a potential mate? Do they understand what they are saying? As the relationship begins to grow, the big question of trust comes up.

When you communicate with intent, you can use your body language to create trust with other people more quickly and in a reliable way instead of leaving up to the unconscious mind. This is an excellent skill for a salesperson, but professional speakers can use it as well. The audience wants to trust the person they see on stage, and being able to do this will help that audience buy into what the speaker is trying to say.

The best way to improve the odds and speed of trust building is to start mirroring what the other person is doing. This is something that has been studied a lot and is an odd phenomenon. You can look around you and see people unconsciously mirroring other people, and then they quickly agree on things. This is how the body says one another, "Hey, we act the same way; we agree on things; we are both on the same page."

This doesn't have to be unconscious, however. You can consciously mirror a stranger, which will help to improve their depth and rate of trust-building. This should carefully be done, but it is rare for a person to call you out on it unless you start to become hyperactive in your movements and try to mirror every twitch.

How can speakers use this? How can a speaker mirror an audience? There are a couple of ways that they could do this. They can align themselves by walking into the crowd and facing the stage as if they were an audience member. Second, if they are given a chance to interact with them, like a Q & A, they can mirror the person asking the question. Thirdly, they can act something out and ask the audience to participate. It should be relevant, however. The speaker will only create more problems if they make their audience to do jumping jacks for no reason.

Its hard work uses body language consciously for psychological purposes, but the things you get in return by making more reliable connections are worth it.

Furthermore, through the act of reading body language, you will be able to know if a person is lying to you. The last chapter of the book will cover this in-depth, but some standard signals of lies are not making eye contact because they think their eyes will give them away. However, it is interesting to note that there are different signs of lying.

Some people will clear their throats a lot, some change the pitch of their voice, or they stutter. Some may even try to take your attention to something else, or they try to stall the conversation. Foot tapping, face rubbing, looking away, blushing, or raising their shoulders can indicate that they aren't comfortable within the interview. But these are only a few things that we will look at later on.

Body language also helps us to express our feelings clearly. When you start looking at nonverbal signals, it will help you figure out how the other person feels about their words. For example, somebody could say 'yes' to something, but their body language says they aren't interested. This is great for a person in a leadership or managerial position to know who would be best for specific job assignments. If their heart isn't into it, they will likely not do their best.

With job interviews, body language is something of the main factor. If the person shows ease and confidence in their body language, they have a great chance of getting the job. Like we have said, body language can make a person seem uncomfortable or out of control. This will make an applicant appear less confident and comfortable.

When you talk to a person, their body language can tell you if they listen or careless. Leaning forward shows interest. Leaning back might mean that they aren't interested or feel as if they are superior to you. If a person is positioned close to you and leaning forward as they are talking, it could mean that they are trying to talk you into something or dominate the conversation. If a person is talking to you and won't make eye contact, you will come off as uninterested and just wait for your turn to speak. This will make you appear as if you don't care, and they probably won't want to listen to you speak.

Somebody language is easier to interpret than others, and this is simply a fact that you will figure out throughout the remainder of this book.

Body Language in History

Like the "manual rhetoric" of the Roman orators and the general mannerism of the entire body, there are gestures that have been studied since Classical times. During the fourth century BCE in Greece, the upperclassmen kept what was considered a "firm" stance and an unhurried walk where they took long strides. This made them appear as people of leisure, which set them apart from slaves and artisans who always had to hurry to get things done. It also worked to separate them from women as well, who walked unnaturally and took small steps. The courtesans of the time would sway their hips as they walked. In Ancient Rome, strictly controlled and limited gestures made a person look in control, required for orators and aristocrats.

Writings about body language were prevalent during the Renaissance. The 17th century's physiognomists, such as Charles Lebrun and Giovanni Della Porta, organized the facial expressions of different emotions and characters. There investigations on gestures, and the investigations of their contemporaries John Bulwer and Giovanni Bonifacio, were conducted by assuming there was a universal language of gesture and expression that people could assume and understand all around the world.

The chances are that the practical study of nonverbal communication started with actors. This is especially true during the 19th century when silent movies were first shown. Actors learned how to properly display feelings, status, and attitudes by mimicking their characters' body language, which is no small feat.

The amazing things are that it is easy to understand and connect with the character even though there are no words or voices. This goes to show how powerful and relevant body language is.

Who was the first person to study body language and its origins?

Charles Darwin, the father of evolution. He was the first person to start studying animals and humans' body language in the book *The Expression of the Emotions of Man and Animals* in 1872. Through careful observation, he found that humans, much like animals, shared inborn behaviors that everybody used. These cues were able to reveal internal emotions or were able to help communicate with people.

The physical conditions that people had to live in, their bodily movements, and their frequent actions all had some consequence on the structure of their bodies. This was discovered by paleo-archaeologists who used excavated skeletons to offer some thoughts about past body habits. Some modern zoologists and ethnologists, like Desmond Morris, stress the similarities of body movements between animals and humans when expressing dominance, fear, and hostility.

Through his book, he pretty much established the science of body language. The majority of observations and studies made today started with his studies.

The biggest parts of the study of non-verbal communication began, oddly enough, during the 1960s. Since that time, it has become a major part of different sciences like psychiatry, social science, anthropology, and business.

Albert Mehrabian

In the late '60s, Albert Mehrabian performed many experiments to figure out how important gestures and intonation were when sharing messages. He found that about seven percent of our communication took place verbally. 39% of it he called paraverbal, which means tone and intonation, and the remaining 55% was nonverbal. This means that the movement of our body, hands, and other simple gestures is very important in how we communicate.

People sometimes debate these results because it came from a controlled experiment and didn't reflect what would be considered a realistic setting. But it gave Mehrabian a chance to show the words alone will not provide us with enough information to understand a message.

- Intonation

Intonation refers to the varying pitch of a person's voice when they speak. Let's think about the word 'thanks.' This is typically seen as a positive word, right? However, if somebody were to say 'thanks' in a firm or curt tone, how will you feel? You probably don't interpret it positively, and you probably won't believe that they are thankful at all. Intonation is a big part of how we convey emotions.

Facial expressions and intonation tend to be very similar across cultures. You can pretty much figure out when a person is disgusted no matter where you are in the world. Similarly, happiness and sadness are typically the same as the world over.

- Gestures and Movements

Gestures are a person's way of conveying the subtle parts of a message. Gestures can even take the place of entire words. For example, if you want a person to continue talking because what they are saying is interested, you won't cut them off and say, "That's cool! Keep talking." You will likely lean forward to let them know you are interested in the things they are saying, or you can nod your head. Most of our gestures involve our hands. In the US, hello tends to be said with a wave. A thumb up is used to say everything is good, or, if a person were to become extremely upset, we could use our middle finger. We can even display impatience with our hands.

Differences in Cultures

The modern study of body language is based on assuming that gestures aren't universal or natural. Instead, they are the products of culture and social influence. The likeness between the facial expressions of chimps to show fear and subordination and the smile of a human can show the difference and the similarities between two primate species.

Anthropologists, like Marcel Mauss, have shown that even the smallest parts of physical activity, like how a person sits, walks, sleeps, or eats, seem to be affected by their culture and vary between societies. This includes deliberate signals people use for communication and involuntary reactions, like weeping or blushing.

Actions that may seem as intuitive or spontaneous, when looked at closely, are not transparent or spontaneous. To some degree, they are ordered, formalized, and stylized to a certain code, meaning nothing in different cultures, places, or contexts. The person she leaps to her feet, smiling, and hugs another person may create some type of discomfort or offense to a person who isn't familiar with this type of greeting. The action of simply nodding the head as you walk past may not have the same effect on a person who isn't used to displaying public acknowledgments.

Modern Studies

The majority of people who study body language are social psychologists, linguists, and anthropologists. The science of body language is kinesics. Their studies include the ways and frequency with which others touch people when they talk and the distance they have during their interactions. Linguists have called gestures as another form of language, possibly even the predecessor of language. They have studied several forms of kinesics communication used by different groups and cultures, like clergy, stockbrokers, and beggars.

Body language provides information that you can't get anywhere else in communication. Movements and expressions can modify, amplify, subvert, and confirm speech. It expresses meanings that may surpass or elude speech. This provides us with a way to see the inner emotional and psychological state of the speaker. Many years before Freud, early writers on decorum talked about slips shown through unintentional body movements, which would undermine or contradict the things they said.

Gestures are unique to the different rites and codes of various cultures. This means body language is important to fundamental assumptions and values. It gives a person a chance to move from nature into their culture through the demeanor and gestures they use to express meaning, whether inadvertent or deliberate. There are many formal contexts where the speaker's movements and posture are more important than their words. Body language plays a big part in non-literate or semi-literate societies where they make commitments through ritual actions and other symbolic objects.

Shame and Purity

There are theories they try to explain why variations or changes in the body language take place. During the 1930s, Norbert Elias, a sociologist, suggested his argument based mostly on European Protestant sources. He suggested that after the freedom in the Middle Ages' body language, early modern Europe had an increase of inhibition with their bodily impulses. This was seen in a rise in shame or embarrassment around physical movements, and a bigger concern over the control or restraint of actions and expressions of emotions.

Mary Douglas, an anthropologist, has argued that with most societies, the body is a social relations symbol, and controlling the body according to society's customs is more or less strict according to the peer pressure a person feels.

Surveys across cultures show the variability of gestures and expressions are supplemented by what travelers experience when they go to different countries or even things seen in movies and heard in music from different world areas. There is a chance that with long-distance travel in the late 20th century and the globalization of culture, some differences have started to diminish. The homogenization of cultures can happen quickly in different aspects, like fashion, foods, or using foreign words or decorations. But it takes more time when it comes to gestures and expressions, which people take longer to absorb and change.

Body language is not only the most fundamental form of expression used by humans, but it is also a very sophisticated and culturally specific form of signals where movements and expressions play as much a part as speech. It groups in the infant grimaces of distaste to an unpleasant sensation, the time of bows between Japanese people of equal rank, and the series of insulting hand gestures that altercating drivers share in Brazil.

Difficulties of Body Language

The people of America and Britain have similar body language, so people will find it easy to read each other. There can still be some regional differences, but it still isn't that hard to figure certain things out. But, for those of use from America or Britain, we would likely have a bit of a probably trying to understand other countries' nonverbal language. If you went to Croatia and waved at somebody, you may be met with looks of scorn or worse because to them, that's offensive. They think it looks too much like a Nazi salute. Luckily for us, we have Google. If you plan to travel to other countries, doing a quick search for offensive body language may be a good idea and could keep you out of trouble.

Meeting Somebody

First impressions are some of the most important parts of meeting something or starting a relationship. A person makes their first impression quickly when they meet somebody. A person has made their first impression within the first 30 seconds of a conversation. The wrong types of body language can create a false impression because people pay attention to the nonverbal language before listening to what you say.

When you learn how to interpret body language, it will help you read people and improve your first impressions. First impressions depend completely on the nonverbal cues. Positive impressions typically involve:

- Keeping appropriate eye contact.

- You are not searching for the room with your eyes.

- We are focusing on the other person.

- Eye contact should not feel like a staredown.

- Standing straight with your chest centered and shoulders back.

- Pay attention to what the conversation is focused on.

People who are looking to establish a good relationship will make sure that they keep an open posture. They will regularly show the inside of their palms, which lets the other person know that they are welcome. What they are saying is important.

The trick about this is if you want to make a good impression, you also have to feel it on the inside. If you plan on showing complete integrity on the outside, you have to make sure you feel it on the inside.

We're going to walk through the small little things you should look for when you first meet a person. The slight movements, body position, and gestures of a person can let you know whether they really what to be talking to you and so much more. You can also use this information to make sure that you make a good first impression.

Handshake

Think back to grade school when you were taught how to shake hands "correctly." You were supposed to have a firm, hard grip. Nobody likes to be handed a fish when shaking hands. It doesn't matter if you're an important person or well-educated; those few seconds it takes to shake hands can tell the other person more about you than any college degree ever could.

All over the world, a handshake is a way to say hello. While it can look like a simple, friendly gesture, it can also cue you in on their personality. This is why it is important to understand the meanings of handshakes in certain situations.

Handshakes start a conversation in almost any type of gathering. This can end up making or breaking the feel of the environment. A study published in the Journal of Personality and Social Psychology explained that people should pay attention to how a person shakes hands. People make judgments and opinions based on this.

During 2000, the University of Alabama conducted a research study where they studied the handshakes of 112 people and compared the impressions they created with the paperwork they had to fill out.

It was discovered that a firm handshake was connected to traits like extroversion and being open to things. Weak handshakes were most connected to higher levels of shyness and anxiety. The women tended to have weaker handshakes than the men, but women who had a firm handshake were positively rated. No matter what sex a person is, strong handshakes equaled a strong personality.

The factors they used to judge the handshakes were complex. The people asked to judge underwent a month of training and were taught to look out for eight things:

- Temperature
- Completeness of grip
- Dryness
- Duration
- Texture
- Strength
- Vigor
- Eye contact

That's a lot to think about when all you want to do is shake their hand and figure out what their personality is like. The easy thing about this was that all of the characteristics related to one another, and all it boiled down to people looking at firm, weak, positive impression, and weak impression. Those who maintained eye contact, held firm, shook with vigor and had warm, strong hands were seen with positivity. That means that if a person has a firm handshake, they have all of the other characteristics.

The lead of the study, Dr. William Chaplin, believed that a person's handshake remains the same throughout their life and lines up with their personality. Body language experts aren't as positive. They think that even if you are shy and introverted, you can do things that will show you have strength behind your nerves.

Besides ensuring that you hold on and pull tight, the body should stay facing the other person to show them that you listen and open to them. Shaking hands while standing will always come off more positively, but you need to maintain eye contact. It is also seen as rude if a person reaches for a handshake from a person who has their hands full. When at a party or gathering, make sure your drink is kept in your left hand so that your right-hand remains warm and dry.

- Offering A Handshake

According to some cultural norms, a person of higher standing, such as a teacher or elder, should initiate a handshake and not the person of lower standing. If the two people are equal in their age and job, offering the handshake makes you appear confident, and you shouldn't be surprised if the other person initiates one.

If you watch world leaders shake hands, try to figure out which one appears to be more relaxed and confident. As a rule of thumb, if you are on the left in pictures, people will view you more positively because standing on the right places you in a submissive stance. The person on the left has the upper hand because their right hand can be seen.

- The Pressure

Ensuring that the pressure you use while shaking hands is just as important as the shake itself. Men will often squeeze harder during a handshake, especially when trying to make a deal, show they are confident or provide a warm greeting. When it comes to pressure, a person should make sure they have the right squeeze for the situation. Keeping a firm handshake, without breaking the other person's hand, makes a person seem confident because limp handshakes can't build rapport.

- The Noodle

Handshakes that you can barely feel show the person has a weak inner-being. When a person uses this type of handshake, it typically shows that they have low self-confidence. Certain people believe that they must be "gentle" when shaking a woman's hand, but that isn't the case. Females read handshakes the same as men, and a weak handshake, no matter the reason, will make you come off looking weak.

- The Dominant Handshake

The opposite of the last handshake is the crusher. This is the handshake that is too powerful, and it could mean that the person is trying to overcompensate for something. This could cause people to dismiss a person.

- The Politician

This is the two-handed handshake where the initiator uses both hands. The handshake is performed like normal, but the initiator places their free hand to top. This is meant to show the other person that they are honest and can be trusted. This isn't a handshake to show power. If their free hand touches your elbow, then they are letting you know they like you.

- The Fancy Shake

There are some people who that a handshake should be cooler. When a person starts adding extra things to a handshake, like a fist bump, they appear immature and unaware. This type of handshake is perfectly normally between friends.

- The Lingerer

This person holds the handshake just a bit too long for comfort. When a person holds too long, it shows that the person seems desperate. Handshakes should only last about two seconds.

- Too Fast

While lingering too long in a handshake is bad, you also don't want to end it too quickly. This would mean the same things as a person who brushes you off. A short handshake makes the person seem rude and don't care or have the time. It may also mean that they are nervous.

- Look Away

Handshakes aren't just about the hands. A person needs to make sure that they make eye contact and smile. A person who is lacking in eye contact will make them look insecure, shy, or suspicious.

- Stare Down

Too much eye contact that makes the other person feels like they are being stared down shows aggression. If the handshake lingers too long, it shows more aggression. Pursed lips and squinted eyes show aggression as well.

- The Perfect Handshake

A perfect handshake means that the palms touch, and the thumbs gently wrap around one another. The grasp is firm but doesn't crush the person's hand. Eye contact is maintained and is warm and soft. This shows the person is friendly and sincere.

Body Orientation

I want to take you on a bit of visualization. Imagine this, you are at the grocery store, and you see a person you went to high school with at the other end of the aisle, and you decide to say help. You turn and walk back to him. Yes, you have your back turned towards him, just hang on for a second, there is a point.

When you get closer to him, judging by the shadow that you see on the floor, you say, "Hi Steven. What have you been up to?" This will freak him out when he turns around, but it shows how important body orientation is. You could stand there and continue to talk to him with your back, but it would be pretty much impossible to hold a conversation.

There is an unwritten rule of keeping the correct body position when you have a conversation with a person. The body will naturally turn to the things you want.

You are likely thinking, "I already knew that. So what? If I need to get something out of the cabinet, I face the cabinet. You face the TV when you watch television." It's no big deal, right? This is an example where an important piece of information gets taken for granted.

During a conversation, we will turn towards the person we want to engage with. The way we keep our body-oriented shows a lot about the things we are interested in. When two people are talking, you can figure out how involved they are by looking to see if they are parallel.

When two people are talking, they face each other and keep their shoulders parallel to each other. This creates a closed formation. This position means that they are physically and psychologically rejecting all of the other people around them to focus on each other. This is probably something you have intuitively spotted before but think about this in a group setting with more than two people.

When there is a group of people talking, you can spot the more interested people in each other by looking for people who are standing parallel. If you see a conversation between three people and two of them are standing parallel, it would be easy to assume that they are trying to push out the third person, or the third has partially removed themself from the conversation.

There may be a chance that the third person wants to join the conversation, but it a part of a different group. If you try to draw a straight line from one person in the direction they are pointed, you will reach another person that they are interested in and want to engage with.

Now, when that third person tries to join in a conversation with two visibly parallel people, two things could happen. That person is either going to be rejected or welcomed.

How can you figure out what is going to happen by watching their body language?

- Welcomed

If the third person is welcomed into the conversation, the other two will need to change their position to allow them in. They are starting in a parallel position, focused on each other, but as the third person comes in, they will both have to give a bit of attention to him. They have to switch up their orientation to redistribute their attention.

They should use both pivots to stand at a 45-degree angle to each other so that they form a triangle. This gives everybody in the group equal attention. If two people are talking and standing at a 45-degree angle, it could mean that they are looking for another person to join their conversation, or they aren't that interested in each other. They will gladly let a third person join their conversation.

- Rejected

What if they don't want that third person in their conversation? When the third person approaches them, they will look over at him to reply to whatever he may have said, but they don't open up their body orientation to let him in. They are trying to reject him, at least at this moment.

It doesn't mean that they hate him; they simply don't want somebody interrupting their conversation. They are nonverbally letting him know, "We are in a private conversation, please leave us alone." For the most part, the person will take the hint and walk away. If they are desperate, though, the third person may try to force his way in.

This can be spotted in several group settings, and it doesn't just include groups of three. The more people you have talking to each other, the more circular the group will turn so that all of their attention is distributed. If people don't have their attention equally distributed, there are likely some outcasts in the group.

Now, there are a few caveats you have to on the lookout for. If you spot people who are talking that aren't parallel to one another, that doesn't mean that they aren't interested in each other. If they are walking or doing something that requires them to move, having this non-parallel position doesn't always show non-involvement.

People are also viewed as aggressive if they walk right up to another person, so this is why most of us will approach people at a

45-degree angle so that we come off as more positive, and there is a better chance of being accepted into the conversation.

To know whether or not two people in a non-parallel conversation aren't interested in one another, there are other things that you have to look at. For example, if they are looking around the room and aren't talking much, then there is a good chance they aren't into each other.

Their Walk

You are sitting in a bar, and somebody walks in like John Wayne. This person likely looks confident and tough. Then again, maybe not, you could view them in a less polite light. No matter what you view, you would find it hard not to jump to conclusions based on how he is walking.

During the last century, psychologists have started to look at these assumptions, and they found that everybody makes these assumptions based on the walking style of a person. After we see the wannabe cowboy walk inside, there is a good chance that we will agree on his personality.

But would this be an accurate assumption? What type of characteristics can be inferred from how a person walks? This may not be what you want to hear, but a psychopath is the best person to ask about walking and assumptions.

We're going to take a look at the connection between gait and personality. One of the earliest investigations was performed by Werner Wolf, a German psychologist, and was published in 1935.

He recorded eight people walking as they played a ring-throwing game. He had them all wear overalls to conceal personality giveaways.

He had all of the participants watch the recordings, which he had edited to hide the heads. Everybody made their interpretations of each other's personalities' based on the way they walked.

The study had some interesting details. For example, they played the metronome to cover up the sounds of the recording. Wolff had believed that the volunteers would easily come up with an impression based on their walking style, and most of the other people would agree. These are a few statements that the volunteers made about "Subject 45:"

- "Dull, somewhat subaltern, insecure."

- "Inwardly insecure try to appear secure to others."

- "Conscious and intentional vanity, eager to be admired."

- "Somebody who wants to gain attention at any price."

- "Pretentious, with no foundation for it."

It's pretty amazing how they were able to come up with similar impressions. They had only a small sampling of people, and there isn't any certain way to know that they didn't pick up on some other cues because the study has its flaws. Plus, the people who participated in the experiment already know each other.

The experiments that are performed nowadays are more sophisticated. They can now use digital technology to bring a walk down to nothing more than a point-light display on a black background using white dots to display the movement of the joints. This removes possible cues.

- A Swaying Walk

Using the black screen and white dots approach, during the late 80s, US psychologists found there are two types of gait, which could be described as a youthful or older movement. Youthful movement involves a bouncy movement, the sway of the hips, large arm swings, and frequent stops. Older movements are slower and stiffer with a forward lean. What's interesting is that their walk didn't always correspond with their age. A person could be young, yet have an older gait and vice versa. People also assumed that people with a younger walk were more powerful and happier. This stayed the same even if their age was apparent by showing their body and face.

This also showed how people made consistent assumptions based on people's walking style, but they didn't look to see if the assumptions were correct. To find this out, we need to look at a British and Swiss study from a few years back. They had the people rate their personalities first and compared the assumptions others made based on their walking.

They also came up with two main styles of walking, and they simply described them differently. The first walking style is loose and expansive, seen as a sign of warmth, trustworthiness, extraversion, and adventurousness. The second was relaxed and slow style, which people saw as emotional stability. But, the judgments based on the walks were wrong. The assumptions didn't match up with what the walker said about their personalities.

- False Assumptions

Our message is that we treat a person differently by their walking style just as much as we do base upon their clothing, accent, or looks. This is used as an information source to figure out what kind of person they are. The assumptions made on a person's face tend to be more accurate than the assumption based on their gait.

At least, that is true for the majority of the judgments made based on gait. But we can make a more accurate judgment in a much more sinister way, and it is based upon vulnerability.

In early findings, it was discovered that women and men with a slower walk, smaller arm swing, and shorter stride were seen as vulnerable. In a Japanese study published in 2006, they asked several men how likely it would be to inappropriately touch or chat up different females based on their walking styles depicted using point-light displays. The only information they had was their walk, and the men said that they would be more likely to approach a woman who appeared more vulnerable, like coming off as emotionally unstable or introverted.

Worse, prisoners with high psychopathy scores are more accurate at spotting people who have been attacked before simply by watching some video clips of them walking. Some prisoners already knew they had this ability. Those who scored highest in the psychopathy scores stated that they often paid attention to how people walked when making a judgment. For example, Ted Bundy is reported having said that he pick out a victim by the way she walked. Now that we know this, let's break down walking styles and what they mean to make accurate judgments.

1. The Driver

This person walks with their weight forward and with a quick stride like they are charging forward. These people will sometimes multi-task when they walk, such as talking on the phone. They are great at finding a way around an obstacle. They don't mind bumping into people if they have to.

This person has a lot of positive traits. They are great at getting things done, are productive, logical, and intelligent. They sometimes come off a little cold. They are fiery and competitive, and this can sometimes be their downfall.

This is the most common walk you will see. You may notice a combination of these in some people, but it does give you another way to read what type of person you are dealing with.

2. The Influencer

This person walks with their head held high, shoulders back, and chest out. They also walk quickly with springiness to their step. They like to engage with people they walk past and will often smile, make eye contact, wave, or shout "hello."

Many celebrities and politicians walk this way. These people tend to be socially adept, charismatic, and fun, but they tend to come off as a bit much. They are often over-the-top and hog the spotlight, and they will sometimes take it from others when they shouldn't.

They may come off as a bit much, but ultimately, they mean well.

3. The Corrector

This person walks light on their toes and keeps their eyes down on the floor. Their pace is cautious and slow as if they are afraid of stepping wrong. They keep their arms close to their side to make sure they don't intrude on others' space. They don't use a phone when they are walking, nor do they interact with friends or others unless they must.

This person is likely polite and introverted. They follow the golden rule of treating others as they want to be treated. Since they are introverted, they don't verbally communicate the things they need or want. They sort of expect people just to know. This can sometimes make them annoyed with other people, making you confused by their irritability.

You should expect them to be fairly quiet, and it shouldn't come as a surprise if they act like you are supposed to know exactly what they want.

4. The Supporter

This person walks with their weight over their legs, not back or forward. They keep a medium-pace, and their movements are very smooth and never choppy. They will engage and gesture to people while they walk, and they like making eye contact instead of shouting or waving.

These walkers are often interested in people rather than tasks, and they like enjoying their personal life more than work. They like being a part of a group and do well within a family system or a team.

They like to be acknowledged for the things they do, but they won't admit this. They are easily distracted.

If you want to impress them, give them a call or send them a card. They have a lot of good qualities, but some people may view them as weak. They have to work hard to stay focused.

5. The Arm Crosser

A person who walks with their arms crossed likely feels vulnerable. If you, yourself, walk this way, you may want to correct this, especially if you are a woman.

Females often cross their arms if they are walking alone at night or in a rough area that they aren't familiar with. Attackers are more likely to prey on people who appear weak, so keeping your arms uncross and standing upright with a quick pace is safer.

6. The Arm Swinger

The latissimus dorsi, a muscle, connects our lower back and arms, and because of this muscle, our opposite arm swings when we take a step to help support the low back. The bigger a person's arm swing is, the healthier of a lower back a person has.

If a person has one arm that moves more freely than the other, it could indicate that they have a neck or back problem due to inactivity or injury.

7. The Stomper

If a person constantly stomps their feet on the ground when they are walking, it sends a signal to their brain about where their limbs are positioned. This could signal that the person has a medical condition. Haydn Kelly, a podiatrist, says that it could be impaired proprioception due to a loss of sensation.

A person who has to stomp their feet when they walk may have a vitamin B12 deficiency, causing tiredness, a sore tongue, and bleeding gums. This would mean that their stomping doesn't show aggressiveness if it happens all the time.

8. The Shuffler

A person who shuffles when they walk doesn't mean they are lazy. Instead, it could mean that they are afraid of falling because of the change in their orientation or depth perception. This is very common for older adults, but anybody can walk like this. Shuffling feet can end up creating other medical issues.

9. The Multi-Tasker

When you see a person walking as they chew gum, take, or any other type of combination, it lets out positive energy. This can help a person if they are feeling low in energy as well. If you start to walk around the house while cooking or talking or organizing, it can help provide you with a boost in creativity. If a person often walks like this, it shows that they are very imaginative.

If you see a person walking and talking on the phone and then they all of a sudden stop, the conversation has become more serious. People will often stop walking and maybe even sit down if the conversation becomes serious.

Arm Movements

No matter if you cross your arms to protect yourself or open them up to welcome a person in, the way that the arms are positioned will provide you with much information when you pay attention.

Different types of arm positions will make different types of moods. When arms are crossed, it means the person is holding in their feelings and keeping others out. Arms help people create roadblocks that others can't move past. If you stay in a position for too long, you will realize that you feel shut out and negative. If a person is in a cold place, keeping their arms crossed is a completely normal activity.

When it comes to contact, touching can be therapeutic if you think about how, where, when, and whom to do it, too. If you touch a person correctly, it can help you engage. It can easily become ugly if it is done wrong. Let's go through some of the different signals you should pay attention to when you meet a person.

- Barriers

Trying to find a barrier to hide behind is normal, and we learn this skill at a very young age to protect yourself. Children often hide behind anything that appears to be solid, such as a parent, couches, or table legs if they start to feel threatened in some way. As we get older, this turns into more sophisticated actions because it becomes unacceptable to hide behind solid objects. This is why we begin to cross our arms if we start to feel threatened.

This continues to develop throughout our adulthood to the point that others don't even notice it. By crossing one or both arms over our chest, we create an unconscious barrier to try and block other things that we don't like or view as threatening. We fold our arms like this because it protects the lungs and heart; we want to protect these vital organs from attack.

Chimps and monkeys also cross their arms to help protect against a frontal attack. This means that if a person walks up to you with their arms crossed, you can guarantee that they have a defensive, negative, or nervous attitude.

- Object Barriers

If a person places a laptop, a cup, or any other object between them and you, they are trying to create a protective barrier. These are subconscious efforts to conceal their insecurity or nervousness, whether they are aware of it.

If you are somewhere where they are serving drinks, people will hold their cup in front of them in both hands to create a barrier that they can hide behind.

- Facing Cross Arms

There has research performed into the gesture of arms crossed, and it has found some interesting results. In one study, a group of students was asked to go to a lecture series where they had to sit with their arms and legs uncrossed through the whole thing. Afterward, they were tested to see how much they ended up learning and the views that they had created towards the speaker.

They asked another group of students to go to the same lecture, but they were told to have their arms crossed.

They ended up discovering that the ones they had to keep their arms crossed learned 40% less than the one that kept their arms uncrossed. The second group had created more critical opinions of the lecturer and lectures and found the lecturer to be less credible.

Years ago, another study was performed similarly with 1500 lecture attendees, and they had almost identical results. They discovered that those who sat with their arms folded created negative impressions about the speaker, and they didn't pay attention to what was being said. This is why many training centers have chosen to use chairs with armrests so that the attendees can be comfortable with their arms uncrossed.

- o It's Comfortable
- o You can ask people about why they have their arms crossed, and many will say it comfortable. The truth is that any gesture will feel comfortable only if you have the right attitude. This means that if you feel nervous, defensive, or negative, having folded arms will feel comfortable. If you are out with your friends having, then folded arms aren't going to feel right.

With anybody's language, the message it sends depends on the sender and receiver. You might feel "comfortable" if you have your arms crossed with your neck and back stiff, but studies have found that other people negatively react to these gestures. So, this means that not only does another person having crossed arms mean that they are already in a negative headspace, you should also try to avoid crossing your arms if you want to show others that you agree.

o   Gender Differences in Crossed Arms

The rotation of our arms depends on our gender. Men's arms will rotate slightly inward, but a woman will rotate slightly outwards. This slight bodily difference is why the mean can throw more accurately, and women have a more stable elbow to hold a baby. Interestingly, women tend to have their arms open when a person is around them that they view as attractive, and they cross their arms if they don't think a person is attractive.

o   Over The Chest

Both arms crossed over the chest, create a barrier to block a person they don't like. There are many different arms-folded positions that people can take that mean slightly different things. With the arms over the chest, this gesture is universal and should be read with the same negative or defensive meaning in nearly every country. Strangers in a public meeting use this; people in queue lines will do this as well. Any place where a person feels insecure or uncertain.

Many people will make this gesture when they disagree with what a person is saying. Speakers who haven't picked up on this position in their listeners won't communicate their message. The experienced speaker knows that they need to use an ice breaker to get their audience into a receptive position so that their attitude moves from negative to positive.

When a person takes this position, it may be safe to assume that they have said something they don't agree with. It could be pointless to continue with your argument even if they verbally agree with you. Body language can be trusted more than words.

You need to figure out the reason for the crossed arms and try to get them into an open position. Their attitude creates this gesture, and then keeping the gesture keeps the attitude around.

A good way to try and get a person to release this arms-folded position is to ask them to hold something or give them a task to perform. If you provide them with refreshments, brochure, or pen, it makes them have to uncross their arms and lean towards you. This places them in a more receptive position.

Asking them to lean forward so that they can look at a presentation can be an effective way of opening them up. Alternatively, you can also lean forwards, keeping your palms face up, and then say, "I noticed that you might have a question. What do you want to know?" Then sit back so that they can see that you want them to talk. When you have your palms face up, you show them that you would like them to be honest with you.

Negotiators and salespeople are taught that they shouldn't continue with a presentation until they have unfolded their arms. Buyers often already have created some sort of object that a salesperson probably won't discover because they didn't notice their arms.

A person who has their fists clenched and their arms crossed over their chest shows hostility and defensiveness. If this is coupled with clenched teeth or a tight-lipped smile and a red face or verbally say something aggressive, a physical attack could be imminent.

- o Gripped Arms

This gesture is where a person tightly grips their upper arms with their hands. This is to reinforce their self and avoid exposing the front of their body. Some will grip their arms so tight that their knuckles turn white. This is a form of a self-comforting hug. This is often seen in people in a waiting room or for traveling by plane for the first time. It shows that they have a restrained, negative attitude.

- Employees and Employers

Status often influences crossed arms. A person who is higher in their social class can make their preeminence known by keeping their arms unfolded. This tells people, "I'm the one in control."

Let's say that you are at a company function and your manager is introducing new employees. He shakes their hand and then steps back to a normal spacing after introductions have been made. His hands will then go down by his sides, in his pockets, or behind him. Rarely does he ever fold his arms over his chest so that he never shows nervousness?

But, once the new employees shake his hand, they may fully or partially cross their arms because of the apprehension of being in a manager's presence. Both the new employees and the manager feel completely comfortable with the gestures they have chosen as the signal of their status.

How do you think things would play out if a manager comes up to a new, confident employee who thinks he is just as important as the manager? There's a good chance that after greeting with a strong handshake, he steps back and crosses arms and keeps his thumbs up.

The thumbs pointed up gestures show that the person feels as if they control their situations. Whenever they talk, they likely gesture with their thumbs to emphasize a point they are making. By having their arms crossed, they create some protection, but having their thumbs up also shows that they are very confident.

If a person feels submissive towards the person they are talking with, or defensive, they will sit symmetrically. This means that both sides of their body will mirror each other. They will appear tenser and will often look as if they are expecting to be attacked. If a person feels defensive and dominant, they will be asymmetrically posed, meaning both sides of their body are positioned differently.

- The Thumbs Up

If you are talking to a person, and they have their arms crossed with their thumbs-up, and they display other positive cues, it might be safe to ask them for a commitment or agreement. But, if they have their arms crossed and keep their fists clenched, you may want to avoid saying anything to them or trying to get them to say yes. It would be a better idea to ask questions to try to uncover their hidden objections simply. When a person has said no, it becomes harder to get them to change their mind without appearing aggressive. When you can read their body language, it will give you the chance to spot their negativity before asking them to verbalize it. This way, you can choose a different course of action.

Historically, people who wore armor or were carrying weapons didn't use these gestures because their armor and weapons protected them.

- The Half Hug

When you were a child, you probably receive hugs from your parents or other caregivers whenever you were in a tough or tense circumstance. As an adult, you likely try to find this kind of comfort when you are in a tough spot. Instead of crossing your arms, which shows anxiety, women will sometimes a half-hug when they only cross one arm over the body and touch or hold onto the other arm. This barrier is often used in situations where a person sees themselves as newcomers to a group or lacks self-confidence.

- The Fig Leaf

This gesture is where they clasp both hands over the lower stomach. If a person is placed into a vulnerable positive, but they know they need to come off as confident and respectful, they will likely stand with their hands clasped over their crotch or lower stomach. You can see this gesture used by politicians and any other types of leaders or people subjected to the public eye. This might be seen during social meetings presided over by an authority figure, like a priest giving a sermon.

Men will hold this position to feel secure by covering their genitals. They are subconsciously protecting themself from an attack. Don't allow yourself to be fooled into believing that this is a natural, confident position. This position feels comfortable because it creates a shield.

This is often a position that people take when they are in line for food at a homeless shelter or receiving unemployment because they feel vulnerable. Adolf Hitler stood like this a lot in public to mask his sexual inadequacy.

- Insecurities of the Important Person

People who are constantly in the public eye, like actors, politicians, and royalty, typically don't want others to notice that they are unsure or nervous. They want to come off as controlled, calm, and cool when out in public, but they still leak out their apprehension or anxiety in some disguised arm-crossing. This works like any other arms-crossed gesture, one arm crosses over in front of the body to the other arm, but they don't fully cross their arms. Instead, they grab hold of a cuff, bracelet, watch, purse, or anything else that is close to their other arm. They are still forming a barrier to feel secure.

Men with cufflinks will often be seen adjusting the cufflinks as they walk across a room where they are on full display of the other guests.

You can spot a self-conscious or anxious man by seeing if you mess with a button, adjusts his watch, checks his wallet, rubs his hands together, or anything else that gives him the ability to reach an arm in front of his body. Business people often go into meetings holding a laptop or briefcase in front of their bodies. To a person who knows what to look for, this is a signal of nervousness because this position doesn't do or show anything else.

You can easily spot these types of things in areas where people have to walk past others watching them. You can't spot a woman's disguised arm barriers as easily as a man's because they often carry a purse that can be grasped to hide their self-consciousness, but it appears as if they are simply holding their purse.

- Amiability

When arms are open, it means that a person is honest, friendly, and receptive. This shows that they aren't hiding anything and that you can easily approach them. This makes others feel comfortable and ease and will draw people in. When people make sure that their body is exposed, it let's other people know that they are open and receptive to whatever has to be said.

Open arms let people know that they are constructive and confident and make the environment more positive. This person is trustworthy, direct, and sincere, as long as their other gestures remain equally forthright and open.

- Embracing

When you are at the airport, watch how family and friends hug when people arrive or depart. When a person hugs on arrival, the embrace is longer than it is when they are leaving. When they first see each other, the hugs are very intense and have a strong embrace. They are bringing each other into their personal space. A departure hug is less passionate and short. It's as if that since they are saying goodbye, they have to release each other.

If a person pats your back when hugging, they are letting you the hug has gone on long enough.

Head

The nod of the head means "yes" in almost every place in the world, and shaking the head means "no." A simple nod is most often used as a nice greeting, especially if people are far away from one another. It simply lets the person know that "Yes, I see you."

The frequency and speed that a person nods with when you are talking with them can share several different messages. A slow nod means that a person is listening closely and is interested in what you have to say. A fast nod means they are telling you, "I've heard enough. I want to speak."

You may have even noticed how some people will nod their heads quickly before they interrupt the person who is talking, and then eagerly make a point.

If you notice that their head movements contradict their words, then you should be suspicious. For example, if they say, "That sounds good," but their head is shaking, then they don't mean what they say.

When a person's nonverbal signals contradict what they verbally tell you, you should always read what the nonverbal is saying because it tends to be more accurate.

- Tilting of the Head

When a person tilts their head, it suggests that they are interested in what you are saying. It's a sign of submission that women often use when they are around a person they like or are interested in the conversation.

If you notice a person tilting their head while you are talking, you should know that they either like you, what you are saying, or both. To find out which it is, change the topic. If their hand remains tilted, then they are likely interested in more than what you are saying.

The head tilt exposes a very vulnerable part of the body. Many canines will lie down and expose their necks when facing a dominant canine to show defeat to end the fit without bloodshed or physical aggression.

When a person tilts their head around you, they are telling you, "I trust that you won't harm me." Interestingly, if you make a point of tilting your head as you speak, the listener will trust what you say. This is why many leadership roles and politicians use the support of the head tilt when addressing people.

People will also tilt their head when they look at something that they don't completely understand, like a new gadget or complex painting. When a head tilt happens in this context, they are simply changing the angle of their eyes to get a better view. Make sure you keep the context in mind.

- The Position of their Chin

The chin in a horizontal position is considered neutral. If the chin is higher than horizontal, they are showing superiority, arrogance, or fearlessness. By raising the chin, the person is trying to appear taller to "look down their nose" at you.

With a raised chin, they are exposing their neck but not in a submissive way. They are, instead, saying, "I dare you to hurt me."

When a person drops their chin below horizontal, it could mean that they are shy, depressed, or sad. They are trying to lower their status and height. This explains the old saying of "hang your head in shame."

A lowered chin can also mean that they are feeling a deep emotion or engaged in self-talk.

When a person has their chin down and pulled back, they feel judgmental in a negative way or threatened. They make themself look as if they have been hit in the chin by whatever it is, causing them to feel threatened, so they have it pulled back defensively. This movement also partially hides the vulnerable neck.

This is a very common gesture when a stranger enters a group. The person who starts to feel as if the stranger is going to steal their attention is more likely to do this.

If a person feels disgusted, they will often pull their chin back because they judge the situation negatively.

- Tossing the Head

This is another submissive gesture used by women when they are around a person they like. They toss their head back for just a second, flip their hair, and then return their head to a neutral position. Besides showing their neck, this is also used as a way to grab attention by communicating the message of "notice me."

If a group of women is talking and then an attractive man shows up, you will likely see the women perform the head toss. Women will also do this to get their hair out of their eyes or face while working on something, so make sure you know the context before you reach any conclusions.

- Swallowing

When a person hears bad news or is getting ready for something that may not be pleasant, you may notice that the front of their neck moves as if they are swallowing. This swallowing is sometimes accompanied by a short closure of their mouth as if they are swallowing.

This is noticeable in men because they usually have a more noticeably Adam's apple. This type of neck movement signals some type of strong emotion. The majority of the time, it signifies fear, sometimes, it shows sadness, but there are times when it could be joy or love.

When a person is weeping or crying, you will likely see this neck movement often. If any situation makes a person wants to cry, however small, it can cause this neck movement.

You will spot this movement right before a doctor tells a family bad news when a person admits that they have made a mistake when a person is afraid that they will get caught, and so on.

People will make this movement when they have tears of joy or tell somebody they love them.

- Nods and Shakes

Nodding movements are a sign of agreement in most cultures and are likely accompanied by smiling and other approval signs. A vigorous nod typically shows strong agreement. A slow nod could mean a conditional agreement.

When a person shakes their head, it typically means that they don't agree or disapprove somehow. The speed of this shake indicates how strong their feeling is. When a person tilts their head down while they shake, it could mean a certain type of disapproval.

When somebody tilts their head from side to side often means "I'm not sure." In Southern India, this movement means yes.

A person that nods their head while you talk shows encouragement and that they want you to continue talking. If they shake their head while you talk shows disagreement, and they may end up stopping you.

A person can use a nod to emphasize their point. This can be a subtle nod or an aggressive and rapid tilt. A quick sharp nod can show a head-butt, meaning that they would like to strike the other person.

Legs

We become less aware of a body part the further away from the body it is. This means that we have more control and awareness over our faces than we do with our legs and feet. It's easy to fake a smile, but think about how hard it is it be consciously aware of what your feet are doing?

This is why you should always turn to the legs and feet to get the true story from somebody and learn the most about what they mean. There can be composed, but their restless foot lets you know that isn't true.

A person's legs will take on four main positions:

1. Parallel

This stance is a subordinate stance where the feet are close together, and the legs are straight. This is a neutral and formal standing attitude. In a school setting, children will often stand in this manner when they speak with their teacher. People who are facing a judge will often stand like this, or if they have to meet with their commanding officer.

When feet are close together, it reduces the foundation and makes the stance precarious. A person can be easily pushed over when they are in this position if caught off guard. Unsure people will often take this stance. With their legs close, they are showing that they feel hesitant.

2. Legs Apart

This is mainly a male gesture and is a stable posture. It shows you that the person is standing their ground. They are showing their dominance. This is where they keep their legs straight and have the feet positions hip-width apart so that the weight is equally distributed between both legs.

Since men have a higher center of gravity, they will adopt this stance more often than women. Besides their height, men take this position more often around other people when using their posture to communicate. It signals dominance by men because it highlights their genitals, which makes them look virile. In sporting events, you will often see men standing in this position.

3. Foot Forward Pose

Between the Middle Ages and the 19th century, the high society men used a stance that would show off their inner leg, which they viewed as an erotic part of the body. They stood where the back leg supported their weight, and they had their other leg kicked out in front of them to show off their inner thigh. The fashion during those times made it more possible to show off their masculinity and legs. You will see celebrities on the red carpet do this.

This is a good indication of what a person's intentions are because we all point our lead foot towards what is on our mind, and this stance also gives the impression that a person is getting ready to walk. When in a group, a person's lead foot points at the most attractive or interesting person, but they will point that foot to the closest exit when they want to leave.

4. Cross-Legged

This is a standing cross-legged position. The next time you are at a meeting where there are men and women, you will likely see some people standing with the legs and arms crossed. If you look a bit more closely, you will notice that they are standing further apart from each other than is customary.

This is how many people will stand when they are around people who don't know all that well. If you took a moment to ask them a few questions, you would probably find out that most of them were strangers until that moment.

Now, when they are sitting, the legs can do several different things. If they have their legs are open, it shows openness and dominance, but if they sit with their legs crossed, it can show that they are defensive or have a closed-off attitude because, symbolically, it denies other people access to the genitals.

As we move away from standing to seated positions, crossed legs are the first thing you will notice. 70% of people who sit with their legs crossed will place the leftover their right. This is a normal position used by the majority of Asians and Europeans.

If a person has their limbs crossed, they are pulling themselves out of the conversation, and it is likely going to be a waste of your time to convince them of something that they have pushed out of their mind.

- Figure Four

If you look down at this seated cross-legged position, it will look like the number. Instead of completely crossing the leg over, they prop it on top of the other leg. This is commonly using among American men. This likely shows a person who feels competitive or argumentative.

While this is less common in Europe, more cultures are adopting it around the world. It is common for men to sit like this to appear youthful and relaxed. In places like the Middle East and parts of Asia, this seated position is seen as an insult because it exposes the bottom of the shoes, which they see as filthy.

Women in pants will often sit like this, but they typically only do it around other women. They don't want to chance to come off as too masculine by doing this around men.

- Leg Clamp

This is a figure four with the hands clasped on the top leg. This shows that they are competitive, and it also lets you know that they are stubborn and will likely reject anything that you try to tell them that goes against what they already believe.

- Locked Ankles

In many-body language studies performed by Henry Calero and Gerard Nierenberg, a person sitting with their ankles locked tend to be hiding information.

Airline personnel is trained to look for this because this shows a person who needs something but is too shy to ask. Apprehensive travelers sit like this, especially at take-off.

In other studies, they looked at patients in a dental office. Of 150 men, 128 of them immediately crossed the ankles when they sat down in the dentist's chair. They would also either grip the armrests or clasp their hands over their groin. They also studied 150 women. Of those, 90 would sit with the ankles crossed and place their hands over the midsection.

- Seated Parallel Legs

The bone structure of women's hips and legs gives them the ability to sit like this to project strong feminine signals. A man can't comfortably replicate this position. When surveyed, men say this is their favorite seated position for women.

- Fidgeting Feet

When a person's feet fidget, they are likely to reach their impatience threshold. Their feet tell you that they want to get away and so they have to fidget until they get the chance to. When standing, repeatedly tapping their foot shows impatience. If seated with their legs crossed, twitching the foot up and down shows impatience.

These are only a few things that you should look for when you first meet a person. The better you get to know them, the more you can infer from their movements.

Falling for a manipulative person can be very detrimental. It could mean that you lose out on a promotion, end up making a bad investment, and find out that your significant other is cheating, or you can be traumatized or physically hurt. When people hear about somebody conning others, they always ask, "How were they able to get away with it? Couldn't somebody stop them?" Yes, somebody could have, and the best way to do that is to stop the manipulation before it causes problems.

To use body language to figure out if a person is manipulative, there are three things you need to do: norm, observe cues, and spot verbal signals.

Norming

Everybody has a baseline on how they act. To norm a person, you have to figure out what their baseline is, or how they are likely to act when at ease. To spot drastic changes in a person's actions that can warn us of manipulation, you must learn to listen to your gut instinct. When you norm somebody, scan across their body and look at:

- Their Feet – Where are the feet angles? Do they have then crossed? How wide are they standing? Feet those are about 12 to 18 feet apart shows confidence.

- Their Hands – Do they have the open or clenched? Are they carrying a weapon? Are they trying to cover a body part? Are they doing something to self-soothe like picking at their nails or ring?

- Their Torso – Is it angled towards or away from me? The direction of their belly button is the best indicator of who has their attention.

- Their Head – What type of expressions are they making? Do they have a narrow gaze? Are their lips pursed? Is their smile genuine or fake?

- Their Tone – When they talk, is it normally high pitched? Are they trying to come off as confident? Do they sound agitated?

- Their Verbal Cues – Why don't they want to give me a straight answer? What was the purpose of the things they said?

Start to get into the habit of watching how people act in a public place so that you can build your norming ability. Once you know a person's norm, you can easily spot sudden behavior changes.

Common Deception Cues

If you were to see a person exhibit these signals, it doesn't always mean that they are manipulative on purpose. However, it can show that they are uncomfortable, nervous, or trying to win somebody's approval. You have to be the one to decide how you want to use the information.

The practiced manipulator will typically go against everything we have been taught. So how can we spot them? Look for people who seem too helpful or an uncomfortably friendly person.

Common cues include:

- Having a false smile. This means that the muscles around the eyes aren't contracted. When a person is truly smiling, the muscles around the eyes will contract and create smile lines.

- The constant mirroring of your body language.

- They keep a deep gaze or strong eye contact.

- They violate your space to try to make some false intimacy like leaning in too close, moving into your bubble even after you move back to reestablish it, and repeatedly touching your shoulder or arm to create rapport.

Chances are when you experience these types of people; there will be a voice inside of you, screaming, "This feels wrong!"

For a person who is unpracticed at manipulating, others may show signs of discomfort. This can include:

- They create some type of barrier using a cup, their arms, books, or any other object they can reach.

- They have unnatural, limited, or stiff body movements.

- They rub their nose.

- They take their fingers and hands up to their mouth to try to "block" their self from telling the truth.

- They avoid eye contact.

- They will self-soothe or self-touch.

If you start seeing these cues in clusters, you should keep a watchful eye out on that person.

Verbal Signals

Now, we need to put everything together that we have learned about our manipulative person. Even the most skilled manipulators will leave us clues. If you are vigilant, you will be able to spot those verbal breadcrumbs that they leave behind.

- Sociopathic Bragging – Master manipulators, or sociopaths, take much pride in all of their abilities, especially those to try and control you. If you listen closely, these people will share information that can save you much misery. Things like "I always get what I want," "I can talk anybody into anything," or "I love controlling people," are all warning signs.

- Discrepancy – The best way to spot manipulation is spotting when a person doesn't match their words and actions up. It is okay to forget different aspects of stories when something is retold, but obvious changes should be red flags that the story is made up of.

- Offering unsolicited help for a price – Have you ever had the misfortune of somebody offering you something for free, you accept it, but then they demand something in return?

People who gain control over you will sometimes offer you some assistance to build rapport and then try to exploit this by "connection" by preying a person's sense of reciprocity. If a person ever says, "Hey, I helped you. Let me in to get a drink," it is a red flag.

- They mumble or change pitch – You know their norm, so intense emotions will change their voice pitch. Manipulators understand that people with a deep voice are seen as trustworthy, so they may try to make their voice deeper to gain trust. A sharp increase in pitch or being monotone can signal that they are nervous.

- Many details – Too many descriptors to prove the truth of what they are saying are typical for manipulators.

- Trust anchors – These are statements that manipulators offer to try and convince a person that they are trustworthy. They will likely seem out of place as well. They say these things because they don't believe you are convinced.

- Absolutes – Manipulators will often avoid giving absolute answers. If you try to ask those questions, they may answer with something like, "Why would you ask me something like that?" "I already gave you an answer," Or "You just don't understand the situation."

The important thing is to make sure that you stay open and aware of these things so that a manipulator doesn't grab hold of you.

How the Brain Affects Body Language

The reason why nonverbal language never lies is that it all happens unconsciously. We can consciously control the things that come out of our mouth to lie or share some half-truth, but the body will still show the truth, but why?

Humans have been communicating nonverbally long before we ever learned speech. We have an ancient system within our brains that understands and conveys all of our emotions and intention through the way we move. This is what is known as the limbic system. It operates exactly. The amygdala is the big player of the limbic system and lives within the medial temporal lobe. It works by helping a person to process through emotions.

We have an exciting evolutionary story that helps to explain how the limbic system came to be. We travel from water-dwelling creatures to land-roaming creatures through the story and continue to the walking, talking, and hunting creatures of today.

Something that we tend to have a hard time believing is that creatures have evolved from common ancestors. These ancient ancestors were water dwellers from 360 million years ago — the changes in climate and the struggle to survive force those creatures to move to the land. Their fins became limbs so that they could walk, and the skin becomes tougher to handle the hard climate.

Around 320 to 310 million years ago, the reptile had evolved. This is where the first parts of the limbic system started to form. The reflexive system of fight or flight and feed and breed started. The section of the brain that this created was made up of the brain stem and cerebellum. The actions of reptiles are very predictable, but it is why they were able to survive. For mammals at the time, emotions weren't a thing.

Once mammals began to emerge, they had a more deliberate social action, unlike those of the reptiles. The main reason for this change could be due to their bonding, habitation, reproduction, nurturing, and change in their metabolism. The offspring of a mammal grows inside of them until they reach a certain stage. They are then fed on mammary secretions, and they have control over the temperature so that they can adjust to various climates.

The new brain structure that developed on top of the reptilian complex is called the cortex. The new section of the brain was made up of the insula, cingulate gyrus, orbital frontal cortex, amygdala, and hippocampus. While mammals were very much superior in their survival techniques to their ancestors, they still naturally used the fight or flight approach, rooted in their reptilian act. Over the years, they learned new ways to work around this fight or flight approach through planning, moving, expressions, and behaviors. Emotions are a very amazing gift and can smell all sorts of different things and be able to remember these things. This is what helped mammals to endure all of their different circumstances. This is the reason why they spread all across the planet.

Then, the common ancestors of humans apes appeared; the primate. There is a possibility that they evolved from mammals that were the most skilled at climbing trees to find shelter and food. The primate's brain created even more complex parts to help these creatures adapt to new social challenges and environments. They had better systems for coordinating movements on the ground and up in trees. They could think and plan things. Their vision even got better, and they were able to recall things.

As the climate continued to change, some primates chose to stay in wooded areas and lived in trees. Others had to start roaming the ground when their trees were turned to brush. These were the primates who began to walk on two legs with their hands-free so that they could farm, hunt, fish, gather food, and make tools. They then began to build and live within fixed shelters.

Their ability to walk on two feet ended up changing their movements and behavior patterns, and how they communicated. Through different gestures, expressions, and sounds, they could express their feelings to all of the other people in their village. Through different civilizations, this continues to be a big part of their communication process and lifestyle. This is what would end up creating social and cultural norms and ethics.

For all of us modern humans, the neocortex is the area of the brain that is the most advanced. All of the other parts of the brain that we have mentioned are still there but are old sections. This new section of the brain is the main reason why we can solve problems, figure out mathematics, navigate through the world, perform introspection, and learn how to speak other languages, use our imagination, and reason about things. This section is also the part that helps us regulate our emotions, control some of our limbic system's impulses, and harbor feelings. The limbic brain is the area that controls all of the nonverbal communication that we do, and we can't completely control this with just our neocortex.

Visual and emotional memory can cause us to act in a certain way that our ancestors likely acted in. We can feel comfortable in favorable places, and then we feel uncomfortable in places where we are in distress or danger. If we find ourselves in threatening situations, we will still act like other reptiles or mammals.

So, nonverbal communication can simply be controlled by paying attention to everything you do because our brain would become too tired. Thus, we are then overtaken by the actions of our ancestors. It is simply easier for our brain to go back to our instincts. While it may be annoying to know that our body will give us away when trying to hide our true feelings, it is just an instinct.

Non-Verbal Body Language

Being able to communicate well is extremely important when wanting to succeed in the personal and professional world, but it isn't the words you say that scream. It is your body language that does the screaming. Your gestures, posture, eye contact, facial expressions, and tone of voice are your best communication tools. These can confuse, undermine, offend, build trust, draw others in, or put someone at ease.

There are many times where what someone says and what their body language says is different. Non-verbal communication could do five things:

- Substitute – It could be used in place of a verbal message.

- Accent – It could underline or accent your verbal message.

- Complement – It could complement or add to what you are saying verbally.

- Repeat – It could strengthen and repeat your verbal message.

- Contradict – It could go against what you are trying to say verbally to make your listener think you are lying.

Many different forms of Non-verbal communication will be looked at within this chapter. We are going to cover:

- Gestures – These have been woven into our lives. You might speak animatedly; argue with your hands, point, wave, or beckon. Gestures do change according to cultures.

- Facial expressions – You will learn that the face is expressive and shows several emotions without speaking one word. Unlike what you say and other types of body language, facial expressions are usually universal.

- Eye contact – Because sight tends to be our strongest sense for most people, it is an important part of Non-verbal communication. The way someone looks at you could tell you whether they are attracted to you, affectionate, hostile, or interested. It might also help the conversation flow.

- Body movement and posture – Take a moment to think about how you view people based on how they hold their heads, stand, walk around, and sit. The way a person carries gives you much information.

Non-verbal communication could go wrong in several different ways. It is very easy to confuse different signals, and the rest of this chapter will make sure that won't happen.

Lower Body

The arms share much information. The hands share a lot more, but legs give us the exclamation point and tell us exactly what someone is thinking. The legs could tell you if a person is open and comfortable. They could also who dominance or where they want to go.

- Legs Touching

When a person is standing, they will only be able to touch their bottom or thighs. This can be done seductively, or they could slap their legs as if they are saying, "Let's go." It might also indicate irritation. This is when you have to pay attention to the context of the conversation. This is very important.

- Pointing Feet

Look at the direction of a person's feet to see where their attention is. Their feet will always point toward what is on their mind or what they are concentrating on. Everyone has a lead foot, and it all depends on their dominant hand. If a person is talking that we are interested in is talking, our lead foot will be pointing toward them. But, if they want to leave the situation, you will notice their foot pointing toward an exit or the way they want to go. If a person is sitting during the conversation, look at where their feet are pointing to see what they are truly interested in.

- Smarty Pants

This is a position where someone tries to make themselves look bigger. They will usually be seated with their legs splayed open and leaning back. They might even spread their arms out and lock them behind their head. This is normally used by people who feel dominant, superior, or confident.

- Shy Tangle

This is usually something that women do more than men. Anyone who begins to feel shy or timid will sometimes entangle their legs by crossing them under and over to block out bad emotions and make themselves look smaller. There is another shy leg twirl that people will do when they are standing. This movement's actual act is crossing one leg over the other and hooking that foot behind their knee as if they are trying to scratch an itch.

Upper Body

Upper body language can show signs of defensiveness since the arms could easily be used as a shield. Upper body language could involve the chest. Let's look at some upper body language.

- Leaning

If someone leans forward, it will move them closer to another person. There are two possible meanings to this. First, it will tell you that they are interested in something, which could just be what you are talking about. But, this movement could also show romantic interest. Second, leaning forward could invade a person's personal space; hence, this shows them a threat. This is often an aggressive display. This is done unconsciously by powerful people.

- The Superman

Bodybuilders, models commonly use this, and it was made popular by Superman. This could have various meanings depending on how a person uses it. Within the animal world, animals will try to make themselves look bigger when they feel threatened. If you look at a house cat when they get spooked, they will stretch their legs, and their fur stands on end. Humans also have this, even if it isn't as noticeable. This is why we get goosebumps. Because we can't make ourselves look bigger, we have to develop arm gestures like putting our hands on our waist. This shows us that a person is getting ready to act assertively.

This is normal for athletes to do before a game or a wife who is nagging their spouse. A guy who is flirting with a girl will use this to look assertive. This is what we call a readiness gesture.

- The Chest in Profile

If a person stands sideways or at a 45-degree angle, they are trying to accentuate their chest. They might also thrust out their chest, more on this in a minute. Women do this posture to show off their breasts, and men will show off their profile.

- Outward Thrust Chest

If someone pushes their chest out, they try to draw attention to this part of their body. This could also be used as a romantic display. Women understand that men have been programmed to be aroused by breasts. If you see a woman pushing her chest out, she might be inviting intimate relations. Men will thrust out their chests to show off their chest and possibly trying to hide their gut. The difference is that men will do this to women and other men.

Hands

Human hands have 27 bones, and they are a very expressive part of the body. This gives us much capability to handle our environment.

Reading palms isn't about just looking at the lines on the hands. After a person's face, the hands are the best source for body language. Hand gestures are different across cultures, and one hand gesture might be innocent in one country but very offensive in another.

Hand signals may be small, but they show what our subconscious is thinking. A gesture might be exaggerated and done using both hands to show a point

- Control

If a person is holding their hand with their palms facing down, they might be figuratively holding onto or restraining another person. This could be an authoritative action that is telling you to stop now. It might be a request asking you to calm down. This will be apparent if someone places their dominant hand on top of a handshake. If they are leaning on their desk with their palms flat, this shows dominance.

If their palms face outward toward another person, they might be trying to fend them off or push them away. They might be saying, "stop, don't come close."

If they are pointing their finger or their entire hand, they might be telling someone to leave now.

- Greeting

Our hands get used a lot to greet other people. The most common way is with a handshake. Opening up the palm shows they don't have any weapons. This gets used when saluting, waving, or greeting others.

During this time, we get to touch another person, and it might send various signals.

Dominance can be shown by shaking hands and placing the other hand on top. How long and how strong they shake the hand will tell you that they are deciding when to stop the handshake.

Affection could be shown with the handshake's duration and speed smiles, and touching with the other hand. The similarity between this one and the dominant one could lead to a situation when a dominant person will pretend they are just friends.

Submission gets shows by placing their palms up. Floppy handshakes that are clammy along with a quick withdrawal also show submission.

Most handshakes use vertical palms that will show equality. They will be firm but won't crush and for the right amount of time, so both parties know when they should let go.

Waving is a great way to greet people and could be performed from a long distance.

Salutes are normally done by the military, where a certain style is prescribed.

- Holding

A person who has cupped hands shows they can hold something gently. They show delicacy or holding something fragile. Hands that grip will show desire, possessiveness, or ownership. The tighter the fit, the stronger they are feeling a specific emotion.

If someone is holding their own hands, they are trying to comfort themselves. They could be trying to restrain themselves, so they will let somebody else talk. It could be used if they are angry, and it is stopping them from attacking. If they are wringing their hands, they are feeling extremely nervous.

Holding their hands behind their back will show they are confident because they are opening up their front. They may hide their hands to conceal their tension. If one hand is gripping the other arm, the tighter and higher the grip, the tenser they are.

Two hands might show various desires. If one hand is forming a fist, but the other is holding it back, this might show that they would like to punch somebody.

If someone is lying, they will try to control their hands. If they are holding them still, you might want to be a bit suspicious. Remember that these are just indicators, and you should look for other signals.

If someone looks like they are holding onto an object like a pen or cup, this shows they are trying to comfort themselves. If a person is holding a cup, but they are holding it very close, and it looks like they are "hugging" the cup, they are hugging themselves. Holding onto any item with both hands shows they have closed themselves off from others.

Items might be used as a distraction to release nervous energy like holding a pen, but they are clicking it off and on, doodling, or messing with it. If their hands are clenched together in front of them, but they are relaxed, and their thumbs are resting on each other, it might be showing pleasure.

- Shaping

Our hands can cut our words into the air to emphasize the things we say and their meaning. We are trying to create a visualization.

If a man is trying to describe the fish he caught during his fishing trip; he might try to show the shape by indicating it with his hands. He might also carve out a certain shape that he wants his ideal mate to be. Other gestures might be cruder when they hold specific body parts and move sexually.

Face

People's facial expressions could help us figure out if we trust or believe what they are saying. The most trustworthy expression will have a slight smile and a raised eyebrow. This expression will sow friendliness and confidence.

We make judgments about how intelligent somebody is by their facial expressions. People who have narrow faces with a prominent nose were thought to be extremely intelligent. People who smile and have joyous expressions could be thought of as being intelligent rather than someone who looks angry.

- Mouth

Mouth movements and expressions are needed when trying to read body language. Chewing on their lower lip might indicate a person who is feeling fearful, insecure, or worrying.

If they cover their mouth, this might show that they are trying to be polite if they are yawning or coughing. It might be an attempt to cover up disapproval. Smiling is the best signal, but smiles can be interpreted in many ways. Smiles can be genuine, or they might be used to show cynicism, sarcasm, or false happiness.

Watch out for the following:

1. Their lips are pursed.

If a person tightens, their lips might be a sign of distaste, disapproval, or distrust.

2. They bite their lip.

People will bite their kip if they are feeling anxious, worried, or stressed.

3. They cover their mouth.

If a person tries to hide a reaction, they might cover their mouth to hide a smile or smirk.

4. Their mouth is turned up or down.

Changes in the mouth that are subtle might be a sign of how the person is feeling. If their mouth is turned up a little bit, they might be feeling happy or optimistic. If their mouth is turned down, they could be feeling sadness, disapproval, or grimacing.

Negative Emotions

The silent signals that you show might harm your business without you even knowing it. We have over 250,000 facial signals and 700,000 body signals. Having poor body language could damage your relationships by sending other signals that you can't be trusted. They might turn off, alienate, or offend other people.

You have to keep your body language in check, and this takes much effort. Most of the time, you may not know that you are doing it, and you might be hurting your business and yourself.

To help you manage your signals, there are several body language and speech mistakes that you can learn to prevent. Here are some mistakes you have to avoid:

1. Not Enough Response

If you are talking with someone, you need to make sure you listen to them. This means you have to smile, nod, and make eye contact. Even if two people don't agree with what they say, you need to let them know that you have heard what they said. This is showing them respect. If you don't do this, you will leave a bad impression.

2. Using the Word "But"

Constantly using the word "but" while you are talking can cause many problems. Most of the time, this will sound like you are just trying to make us some excuses or don't care about what they are saying. You might say: "I am sorry that your product didn't get to you on time, but you know how the weather is." This statement doesn't show you are sorry. You are placing the blame on the weather instead of addressing the real problem.

3. Personal Space

Invading another person's personal space can have detrimental results. One good example is that men always seem to invade a woman's personal space, whether they know it or not. This could cause some harassment lawsuits. The best space to keep between you and others is about one and a half feet. Never treat another person's space as if it was your own.

4. Talking Too Fast

Blinking fast or talking too quickly shows nervousness and distrust. Try to pause between each sentence and let others finish their sentence before your interrupt. Eye contact is very important. If you have a hard time looking people in the eye, look in the center of their forehead. It looks like eye contact without all those uncomfortable feelings.

5. Not Listening

It doesn't matter what you do for a living; you will have to talk with people some time or another. The main thing that will make or break any relationship is not listening. Listening could impact your relationship with employees, suppliers, performance, and scales better than other forms of communication.

6. Slumping

If a person slumps in their seat, they show that they don't have any energy or confidence. It is important to show passion and let others know that you believe in yourself. If you are hunched over or slumping, you are sending the wrong message. If your posture is strong, you will feel energetic, and it will be a win for all people involved.

7. Checking Your Phone

If you are in a public gathering, put away your phone. Everybody is addicted to their phones now, and this is extremely rude. Try engaging with others, and stop checking your phone every few minutes. If you have an emergency, that's fine. It is easier to make connections with others if you don't have things distracting you.

8. Face is Scrunched-Up

You might not realize that your face is scrunched-up or that your brow is furrowed. This can make others think you are intimidating or hostile. You can discourage others from being open, or it might make them get defensive. You can verbally assure them that you understand and support what they are saying.

9. Not Making Eye Contact

I used to work with someone who would immediately stare into space anytime somebody talked to them. They claimed it was easier for them to focus on what others said if they didn't look at who was talking. People might use many different communication types but always make eye contact. Even if you can keep moderate eye contact, it will communicate confidence, interest, and put everybody at ease.

10. Not Smiling

Do you know that smiling can make you feel happy? People like to believe the opposite. If you can keep a nice smile on your face, you will feel more confident, and people will want to work with you. If you realize you want to make a face, turn that face into a smile.

11. Glancing Around

Everybody has encountered someone who will constantly look around while they are talking to you. It probably makes you think that they are trying to find someone else to talk to. Don't be this person. Everyone you talk to needs to be treated with respect.

12. Handshake Too Weak or Strong

Handshakes are normally the first impression that someone gets from you. If your handshake is too weak, it will show you aren't professional, and it might be new to them. If your handshake is too strong, it might warn them that you are too aggressive. Try to find a happy medium so that you will make a good impression.

When you observe other people, you can pick up on their emotions by their Non-verbal signals. These indicators are not a guarantee. Contextual clues might be used, in addition to what they are saying and what is happening around you at the time.

Here are some emotions and how to spot them:

Fear, Anxiety, or Nervousness

Fear could happen when our basic needs get threatened. There are many different levels of fear. Suppose might be mild anxiety or full-blown blind terror. The various bodily changes that get created by fear can make this one easy to spot.

- Voice trembling

- Errors in speech

- Pulse rate extremely high

- Vocal tone variations

- Sweating

- Lips trembling

- Muscle tensions like their legs wrapped around something, clenched hands or arms, elbows are drawn in, jerky movements

- Damp eyes

- Holding their breath or gasping for breath

- Not looking at one another

- Fidgeting

- Dry mouth indicated by licking their lips, rubbing their throat, or drinking water

- Defensive body language

- Face is pale

- Fight or flight body language

- Breaking out in a cold sweat

- Any symptoms of stress

Sadness

- Lips trembling
- The flat tone of voice
- Body drooping
- Tears

Anger

- Clenched fists
- Invading body space
- Leaning forward
- Baring their teeth or snaring
- Using aggressive body language
- Neck or face is red and flushed
- Displaying power body language

Embarrassment

- Not making eye contact
- Looking down and away
- Neck or face is red and flushed
- Changing the subject or trying to hide their embarrassment
- Grimacing
- Fake smiles

Positive Emotions

When you have positive body language, it means that you are interesting, approachable, and open. This isn't saying that you need to use this kind of body language all the time or that it is the best signs that will show a person is friendly. It's just a good beginning point for reading positivity in others as well as yourself.

- Get Barriers Out of the Way

To gain someone's trust, you have to make sure that you aren't coming off as a threat and that you don't see them as a threat. Having defensive body language could affect your attitude. If you are defensive, it will make it hard for other people to accept and approach you.

For this reason, you have to keep an open body language and watch out for barriers.

Your goal needs to be getting rid of your defensiveness and to make a warm, welcoming, and confident atmosphere. Show others that you aren't scared of them, and they shouldn't be afraid of you.

This is a process, and a stranger won't be your biggest fan. If you know what steps to take, you will know their attitude toward you, and this will speed things up.

These are the steps you need to take:

1. A total stranger might have their arms or legs crossed and possibly both. They might stay away from you. They may

also hold things in front of them. They could also button their coat.

2. As they begin to warm up to you, you may notice that they uncross their legs and other barriers begin to disappear. They might even move closer to you.

3. They may start to gesture more and expose their palms.

4. They will uncross their arms.

5. They may point or lean their body toward you.

Taking the initiative might help other people open up to you. Everyone unconsciously begins to copy the body language of others. You can reverse this process by getting into a defensive posture.

How fast this process goes all depends on the culture, character, whether they are an extrovert or introvert, and context such as meeting a stranger on the street versus meeting them at a party.

- Nothing to Hide

Think about a time when you were away from your friends and family for a long time. How did they greet you once they saw you again? Did they spread their arms and expose their palms like they were hugging you from a distance? This open and positive gesture could warm your heart.

Even if you can't use it every day with everyone, your boss might think you have lost your mind or won the lottery. You can use gestures that are similar to show honest, positive, and open body language.

If their palms are faced out, this is a sign of willingness and honesty. This isn't threatening in any way. You are letting others know that you aren't hiding anything, and they can trust you. Here are some signals that could help show sincerity and cooperation:

1. Place your hands in a neutral position. Don't look down on them or bow to their wishes.

2. Make good eye contact. This shows you aren't afraid, but you are attentive.

3. Keep your body open. Don't hold anything in front of you.

4. Stand or sit up straight to show confidence and energy.

5. Smile

- Lean Forward

If a person likes someone, they want to get as close to them as possible. You will seem more interesting if you get close to them. If a person learns, and especially if they are nodding and smiling, they are interested in what you are saying and want you to continue.

Is this saying you always have to lean forward and nod?

No, overdoing this might cause some problems:

1. If you constantly smile and lean with everybody, you will look extremely eager to please. You will lower your status with others.

2. If you lean too far, you could invade their personal space and cause them to feel uncomfortable. This is another

reason we lean forward when we want to intimidate an opponent. This type of lean will be tenser and more aggressive.

Try comparing learning to drive. When you press the gas pedal, the more eager and engaged, you are. If you don't press the pedal, you will appear more relaxed and distant. Don't go toward the extreme because you will need to change your speed for every situation.

Much like with driving, the direction in which a person leans has a big impact. We will lean toward and gesture toward things or places we want.

- Being too Positive

Just because you have positive body language doesn't mean it is good or the best way to communicate. Since we are social animals, we have many emotions and attitudes. If you just try to use only one at a time, you will seem one dimensional or fake.

Expressing positive and attentive attitudes at all times might hurt your status and reputation. People will sometimes begin to take this for granted and will dismiss it. You have to give attention and care to others but only to people who deserve it.

This will hold for anybody who wants to be super nice to people that are dating. How could others take care of you? If you only try to help them but dismiss yourself, you will look boring and shallow. There won't be any tension or excitement.

Non-verbal Signals Used Universally

Non-verbal communication is different for everybody and in different cultures. A person's cultural background will define their non-verbal communication since some communication types, like signs and signals, need to be learned.

Since there are different meanings in non-verbal communication, there could be miscommunication when people from different cultures try to communicate. People might offend others without really meaning to due to cultural differences. Facial expressions are very similar around the world.

Seven microexpressions are universal, and we will go more in-depth about these in a later chapter, but they are hate/contempt, anger, disgust, surprise, fear, happiness, and sadness. It might be different in the extent of how people show these feelings since, in specific cultures, people might readily show them where others won't.

Let's say you are an American and you take a trip to Italy. You don't speak Italian. You don't take a translator with you, and you forgot your dictionary. You have to rely on non-verbal communication to be able to communicate with the people there.

You find a nice quiet restaurant that you want to try, so you point to your selection on the menu. You pay your bill and leave. The workers nod at you as you leave being a satisfied customer.

There might be other times when things might not go due to non-verbal communication like people who don't make eye contact, or they get offended when you do make eye contact.

Nods might also have different meanings, and this can cause problems, too. In some cultures, their people might not say "yes," but people from different cultures will interpret as "no." If you nod in Japan, they will interpret it as you are listening to them.

Here are different non-verbal communications and how they differ in various cultures:

- Eye Contact

Many Western cultures consider eye contact as a good gesture. This shows confidence, attentiveness, and honesty. Cultures such as Hispanic, Asian, Native American, and Middle Eastern don't think eye contact is a good gesture. They think it is rude and offensive.

Unlike Western cultures that think it's respectful, others don't think this way. In Eastern countries, women absolutely can't make eye contact with men since it shows the power or sexual interest. Many cultures accept gazes as only showing an expression, but staring is thought of as rude in most.

- Gestures

You need to be careful doing a "thumbs up" because it is very different in many cultures. Some view it as meaning "okay," but in Latin America, it is vulgar. Japan views it as meaning money.

Snapping of your finger may be fine in some cultures, but it is disrespectful and offensive in others. In some Middle Eastern countries, showing your feet can be offensive. Pointing your finger is an insult in some cultures. People in Polynesia will stick their tongue out when they greet someone, but other cultures see it as a sign of mockery.

- Touch

Touch is thought of as rude in most cultures. Some cultures look at shaking hands to be acceptable. Kissing and hugs, along with other touches, are looked at differently in different cultures. Asians are extremely conservative with these types of communications.

Patting someone's head or shoulder has different meanings in different cultures. Patting a child's head in Asia is extremely bad since their head is the sacred part of their body. Middle Eastern countries think people of opposite genders touching to be very bad character traits.

How and where a person gets touched could change the meaning of that touch. You need to be careful if you travel to various places.

- Appearance

This is a good form of non-verbal communication. Their appearance has always judged people. Differences in clothing and racial differences could tell a lot about anyone.

Making yourself look good is an important personality trait in many cultures. What is thought to be a good appearance will vary from country to country. How modest you get is measured by your appearance.

- Body Movement and Posture

People can receive messages or information from how your body moves. It can show how a person feels or thinks about you. If they don't face you when you are talking, it might mean that they are shy or nervous. It might also show that they don't want to be talking to you. Other movements like sitting far away or near, somebody might show that they are trying to control the environment. They might be trying to show power or confidence.

A person's posture, like sitting slouched or straight, could show their mental condition. Having their hands in their pockets could show disrespect in various cultures. If you are in Ghana or Turkey, don't cross your legs when you sit because this is thought of as offensive.

- Facial Expressions

Our faces show many feelings, attitudes, and emotions. Cultures can determine the degree of these expressions. Americans will show emotions more that people who live in Asia.

Most facial expressions are the same throughout the world, but specific cultures won't show them in public. These meanings are acknowledged everywhere. Showing too much expression could be considered shallow in specific places where others take it as weak.

- Paralanguage

How we speak constitutes what we talk about. Rhythm, vocal tones, pitch, and volume can speak more than what the words are expressing. Asian people can stop themselves from shouting because they have been taught that this is not acceptable.

This is what is known as vocal qualifiers. Whining, yelling, and crying are vocal characterizations that could change the message's meaning. In specific cultures, giggling is a horrible gesture. Many emotions can be expressed through vocal differences, but all of them are a part of everyone's paralanguage.

- Personal Space

People in different cultures will have different tolerances for space in between people. People who live in the Middle East like to be very close when they are talking. Other people might be afraid to be close to other people while they are talking.

Europeans and Americans don't have as much acceptance about people entering what they call their personal space. This is even less when talking about Asians. Everybody will have their own space that they don't want others to enter. There are many cultures where close contact between strangers is acceptable.

How Are They Breathing?

There are different ways you can read someone's body language. It can be read by their leg and arm movements, facial expressions, eye contact, or smiles. Do you realize that how a person breathes has meaning, too?

Emotions and how you breathe are connected. You could read a person's feelings by watching the way they breathe. If emotions change, how they breathe might be affected. See if you can notice breathing patterns in your family, friends, coworkers, or significant other. They may not tell you exactly how they are feeling, and it might depend on certain situations.

- Deep breathing might indicate excitement, attraction, anger, fear, or love

Deep breathing is the easiest pattern to notice. If somebody suddenly starts to hold their breath, they might be feeling a little scared. If someone takes a deep breath and then shouts, they could be angry. Excited people, who are experiencing shock or are surprised, might suck in a deep breath. They might also take in a deep breath and hold it for a few seconds. If their eyes start to glow, this might indicate that they are surprised or excited. A person might start to breathe deeply if they feel an attraction toward another person. You may notice someone take a deep breath in, suck in their stomach, and push their chest out to try and impress somebody they are attracted to.

- Sighing might signal hopelessness, sadness, or relief

When you sigh, you are letting out a deep, long breath that you can hear. Somebody might sigh if they are feeling relieved after a struggle has passed. They are thankful that their struggle is over. A sign might show sadness or hopelessness like somebody who is waiting for a date to show up. It could also show tiredness and disappointment.

- Rapid, heavy breathing might show fear and tiredness

You may have just seen a person rob a place, and the police are chasing them. You notice they are breathing very rapidly. This is because their lungs need more oxygen since they are exerting much energy. After all, they are running. Their bodies feel tired, and their lungs are trying their best to keep up. We feel the same effects when we feel scared. This will happen when we experience fear; our lungs need more oxygen, so we begin to breathe faster. You will easily see when somebody has been scared or running by noticing the way they are breathing.

Another interesting fact about breath is that smells can influence breath. Any odors that are tied to emotions can change a person's respiration rate. Several studies have shown that the body will respond to bad and good smells by breathing differently. If you were to smell something rotten, you would end up breathing in a shallow and rapid manner. But, if, instead, you smelled baking bread and roses, your breath would be slow and long. The really interesting part of this is that the breathing rate will change before the brain has ever been able to consciously register if the smell is good or bad.

According to *Scientific American*, the emotions that we have with smells and scents are extremely associative. We started learning about these different smells in the womb, and then during our lives, our brains learn to refine our views of emotional rewards, pleasures, and threats that are contained within a certain odor. If a person breathes deeply, they feel that something is safe, creating a pleasurable emotional state. This means if you notice a person's breathing rate suddenly changes, let your sense of smell catch up first. It could be that they have gotten a whiff of something they either like or dislike.

The interesting thing is that while we can learn how people feel based on how they are breathing, the way a person breathes can also affect their emotions. In a 2006 study published in *Behavior Response & Therapy,* they discovered that undergraduates who practiced slow-breathing exercises for 15 minutes had a more positive and balanced emotional response afterward than the group faced with 15 minutes of unfocused worrying and attention.

And it doesn't even have to do with just being calm. In a French scientist Pierre Phillipot, he asked some participants to identify the pattern of breath that they connected with certain emotions such as sadness and joy. They then asked a separate group of people to breathe in a certain manner, and then they probed their emotions. The results they got were amazing. If the subjects were told to breathe in a particular manner, even if they were unaware of it, they said they felt the feeling associated emotion, apparently, out of nowhere.

To wrap this section up, I want to share one more way you can use a person's breath to tell how they feel. This is something that you can't readily do, but it is still interesting.

A new idea that is being studied about emotions and breath is that what you exhale also plays a role in emotional response and that the chemically analyzed exhales were able to figure out how the person felts. In an article from *Science News*, the air's chemical makeup within a soccer stadium varies when people begin cheering, and the same is true in movie theaters. They studied 9500 people as they watched 16 different films that ranged from rom-coms to horrors, and then they studied the air composition of the room to see if it changed during certain scenes that were rather emotional in one way or the other.

The crazy thing is that it did. In suspenseful moments, there were more CO_2 and isoprenes in the air, which are chemicals associated with muscles' tensing. Every type of emotion came with its chemical makeup.

Facial Microexpressions

Learning to decode facial expressions is similar to having superpowers. The face, with all its expressions, which are called microexpressions, could be a window into their soul. Knowing how to read them could help you to understand a lot about how someone is feeling.

Methods of Nonverbal Analysis

To perform any nonverbal behavior analysis, you have to use techniques that can help you describe the behavior in a way so it can be trusted. The advantages of scientific analysis are:

- To select a person's weaknesses and strengths during normal relations.

- To expose lies by using a combination of facial and verbal expressions.

- To anticipate a person's behavior.

- To identify another person's state of mind and emotions.

It doesn't take long to learn these techniques with an interactive and focused program based on specific exercises.

Scientific Based

The first text written about emotional expressions was written by a French neurologist, Guillaume Benjamin Amand Duchenne de Boulogne. This text was written in 1862 and demonstrated the method of using electrodes on the facial muscles to establish their relationship between the facial muscles' movements and the subsequent emotional expression. To honor him, a true, authentic smile can sometimes be called the Duchenne smile.

Charles Darwin wrote the Expressions of the Emotions in Man and Animals in 1872. In this, he says that emotions are just another evolutionary product and are inherited. Body and facial expressions go hand in hand with emotions and look to be the same in people who live in different parts of the world and other animals and primates. Darwin's studies didn't continue after he died because of the scientific community's hostility toward his theories and him. He was criticized for saying animals have emotions. According to his critics, only humans can feel things. His methods were based on observations rather than science.

This concept of emotional expressions being universal was discovered one more time in the late 1950s. Researchers like Birdwhistell, Izard, Ekman, Ellsworth, and Friesen tried to validate Darwin's theory. They worked together to develop a set of theories, tests, and methods that created the "Facial Expression Program." They believed the origin of emotional expressions and emotional experiences would be a specific number of inherited neurological programs. We know now that there are specific paths for every emotion that causes a facial expression associated with that particular emotion. According to the theory of evolution, emotions have adaptive functions that will let a human react through immediate responses to various stimuli for survival.

There are two groups of nonverbal techniques:

- Decoding technique: This interprets and will give meaning to movements.

- Coding technique: This describes the body and facial movements.

Facial Expression Techniques

- ISFE or Interpretative System of Facial Expressions

Jasna Legisa developed this in the NeuroComScience laboratory in 2013. It is a table of what facial movements mean. It comprises a set of descriptions and tables that order and integrate facial expressions according to the emotions they are related to. This information was taken from existing literature and previous systems about this subject.

Other than secondary and primary emotional expressions, other facial signs get described as regulators, illustrators, and manipulators. According to Ekman, Izard, and Hjorstjo, emotional expressions get grouped into "big families." These "families" include many facial expressions that, even though they mean slightly different things, get united because they receive the same emotional range. Within the "surprise" family, you will have an annoying surprise, face surprise, a real surprise, awe, and many more.

Primary emotional movements get put into three categories:

- The first category includes muscular movements that belong to specific emotions.

- The second category includes movements that might belong to primary emotions.

- The third category includes minor variations to emotions that could be part of many emotional families.

These categorizations make the interpretation and accuracy of the whole analysis.

- Mimic Language and Man's Face or the Hjorstjo Method

An anatomy professor at Lund University located in Sweden, Hjorstjo, in 1969, tried to systematically categorize certain facial movements with their meanings into eight emotional families. His handbook reports the decoding and coding of facial expressions, so it is possible to determine the facial muscle contractions either in combination or by themselves.

- MAX or Maximally Discriminative Coding System

This system gives meaning to the facial movements instead of just describing them. Izard developed MAX in 1979. Later in 1983, he worked with Hembree and Dougherty to create an advanced version of MAX that was named AFFEX. The created facial configurations based on regular expressions of emotions like shame, disgust, pain, surprise, happiness, interest, fear, sadness, and anger. Basically, for every emotion and expression gets classified.

- EMACS or Emotional Facial Action Coding System

Friesen and Ekman worked to describe the expressions of six emotional families: fear, surprise, anger, disgust, sadness, and happiness. Hager has been working at Ekman's laboratory since 1994, studying facial expressions by using an automatic computer to identify their techniques. This database has created the FACSAID or FACS Affect Interpretation Dictionary system.

- Hanes

During the same year that the first version of FACS was published, the Hanest Manual was also published. The Hanest Manual was created by Gergerian and Emiane, who are two French scientists. It has the same plan as FACS to describe facial movements.

- FACS or Facial Action Coding System

Vincent W. Friesen and Paul Ekman in 1978 introduced FACS or the Facial Action Coding System. In 2002, while working with Hager, they release another version. This one is a descriptive facial coding system, and it doesn't ascribe meaning to facial expressions. It contains detailed descriptions of changes that happen because of facial movements.

- BabyFACS or Baby Facial Action Coding System

The same structure that is used for adults can be used for small children and babies. During 1993, Oster looked at babies' facial expressions and changed up the descriptions as needed. These are only descriptive and don't give any meanings to the emotions.

Reading Microexpressions

Knowing the best way to read and understand microexpressions is important because it helps you read a person's nonverbal actions. Here is a short guide on understanding microexpressions.

Happiness, contempt, fear, surprise, disgust, sadness, and anger are the seven universal microexpressions. These can happen very quickly. Looking at a person's face is the best way to know how somebody is feeling. The bad news is that most of these are usually overlooked. The show *Lie to Me* was based on Dr. Paul Ekman's research. He has conducted numerous studies on how to decode facial expressions. He has proven that all facial expressions are universal.

This means that people who live in the United States will make the exact facial expressions as people who live in Madagascar who hasn't ever seen a movie or television show. People who were born blind will make the same expressions even though they have never seen anybody's face. Ekman designated seven expressions that are used most often and are easy to understand. Figuring out how to read them can be helpful when trying to understand other people. If you would like to practice reading faces, you need to know the basic expressions. It would be a good idea to practice these facial expressions in a mirror so you can see what they look like. You may even realize that if you make the expression successfully, you might feel that same emotion. While facial expressions can cause emotions, emotions cause facial expressions.

- Happiness

The corners of your lips will be drawn up and back.

Your mouth might or might not be parted with your teeth exposed.

There will be a wrinkle that runs from the outer nose to the outer lip.

Your cheeks will be raised.

Your lower eyelid might be tense or showing wrinkles.

There will be some crow's feet on the outer corners of the eyes.

- Contempt / Hate

There will be one side of the mouth raised.

- Fear

Your eyebrows will be drawn and raised together, most specifically in a straight line.

Wrinkles on the forehead will be in the center between the eyebrows and not all the way across.

Your upper eyelid will be raised, but the lower is drawn up and tense.

Your eyes will have the white on the top half showing only. The lower whites won't be showing at all.

Your mouth will be open with the lips drawn back, tensed, and stretched.

- Surprise

Your eyebrows will be raised and curved.

The skin beneath your brow will be tightly stretched.

Horizontal wrinkles go across your forehead.

Your eyelids will be open with the whites show above and below.

Your jaw will be slack, teeth apart, but there shouldn't be any tensions or stretching of the mouth.

- Disgust

Your upper eyelid will be raised.

Your lower lip will be raised.

Your nose will be wrinkled.

Your cheeks will be raised.

There will be lines that show just under your lower eyelid.

You make this expression when you smell anything horrible.

- Sadness

The inner corners of your eyebrows will be drawn in and up.

The skin beneath the eyebrows will be triangulated. The inner corner will be up.

The corners of your lips will be pulled downward.

Your jaw will come up.

Your lower lip will stick out a bit.

This is the expression that is the hardest to fake.

- Anger

Your eyebrows will be lowered and drawn together.

You will have vertical lines between your eyebrows.

Your lower lid will be tense.

Your eyes will be bulging or in a hard stare.

Your lips could be pressed together firmly, with the corners drawn down, or shaped like a square like you are shouting.

Your nostrils might be dilated.

Your lower jaw will jut out.

All three areas of the face have to be engaged not to have any ambiguity.

Once you have practiced these for a while, see if you can spot them in the people you are around the most.

Anyone is capable of telling a lie, and for the most part, everyone does. Most Americans will tell several lies each day. There are ways you can spot these lies.

The best way you can spot a lie is by knowing how a person will act when they tell the truth. Ask anyone you know a simple question such as: "Where are you from?" Now, you need to watch what their eyes do and the way their voice sounds.

Once you have established this information, you just have to look for changes in their behavior in four categories: speech content, facial expressions, voice tone, and body movements. These are all communication codes.

Know that these signs aren't foolproof. If a person feels uncomfortable, they might fidget in their seat. If they feel nervous, their voice might crack.

There has been much debate within the healthcare community, basically in the mental health community, about what body language tips truly show when lying. What we perceive could keep us from correctly interpreting the signs that we see. It's tough trying to figure out people just by watching their body language because someone might look tense or uneasy for many different reasons. It's easy to think that somebody who will not make eye contact with you is automatically lying. They may not be lying, but they might be feeling anxious, ashamed, or bored. We aren't as great as reading people as we think we are.

There is some good news. There are signals that you can look for. Who tells more lies, women or men? Do they have different reasons for lying?

In a study that was conducted with two groups, one group was made up of 77 college students, and the other group was 70 random individuals; they were told to keep a daily diary for one week and write down every lie they told during their social interactions that lasted for ten minutes or more. Students told lies in one out of three interactions. The random community people said they lied one in about every four interactions. After one week, about nine percent of the different community people and one percent of the college students claimed not to have lied at all. Yes, you might be thinking that they are telling lies about not telling lies.

Even though it might be clear that everyone lies, it is clear that there a specific people who can lie easier and more than others. While doing this study, the "champ" told 46 lies in only one week, and this equated to about seven lies each day. You may be wondering who these people are that can lie more than the rest of society. These are people who lie every single day. Do these people possess certain personality traits? What gender are they? What is their age? Does telling lies to have connections to relationships?

A Liar's Personality

While doing the diary study, each person filled out specific personality measures. That information was used to see if certain personality types were prone to telling more lies.

When you went through the questions about "who lies?" did a certain kind come to mind? Did you guess that people who lie more were more cunning and manipulative? If so, you need to remember to use your intuition. People who like manipulating others are more likely to lie than people who aren't as manipulative.

People who are manipulative normally only care able themselves, so you might think that liars don't care about anybody else. This isn't true. People who frequently lie might also care too much about other people. What they care about most is what other people care about them. These people worry about the impression they make on others: "If I do this, will they think I'm a loser?" or "If I say this, what will she think?" These people have a personality type of impression-management. This person is going to tell many lies. What is very interesting about these people is that they know they are lying and know they do it more than other people. This is noteworthy because the participants of the diary study thought they were a lot more honest than other people.

Extroverts will also lie more. This is why we have to keep track of social interactions and not just lies. If we only counted the lies, extroverts could lie more than introverts because they spend much time around others. This allows us to look at lying rates or how many lies people will tell according to their opportunities to lie. Extroverts told more lies than introverts, even if the difference wasn't that substantial.

So, why do extroverts lie more than introverts? It is because little lies will make social interactions go smoother. Extroverts know about being nice to others, and they practice this as often as possible, so they don't realize that they are lying. When extroverts were asked to look at how many lies they told during a week, it surprised them to know how much they lied. The reason isn't clear as to why extroverts lie more than introverts.

The next trait is a responsibility trait measured by the same scale that shows people who are ethical, reliable, honest, dependable, and responsible. Responsible people won't lie as often as people who aren't responsible, especially any lying that serves themselves.

Relationships and People Who Lie Frequently

The people who participated in the above study rated the quality of their relationship with people of the opposite sex and with people of the same sex. They showed how satisfying, enduring, and warm their relationships were, how well their friends and they knew one another, and how quickly they made friends.

The quality of their relationships with people of the opposite sex didn't correspond with how quickly they lied. It was the total opposite when they had relationships with people of the same sex. People who had good relationships with people of the same sex didn't lie as often or as much, especially self-serving lies, than people who had bad relationships with people of the same sex.

How Women and Men Compare

On average, with each type of lie, men and women are equal in their tendency to tell lies. When they looked closer at different kinds of lies and targets, this is when differences showed up.

Think about two kinds of lies: kind-hearted and self-serving.

Kind-hearted lies are told to make somebody else feel or look better or keep from hurting their feelings, blamed, embarrassed, or punished. Look at the following statements:

"I know how you feel!"

"You look wonderful!"

"What a wonderful meal!"

How to look at these four combinations of targets and liars:

1. Women telling lies to women.

2. Women telling lies to men.

3. Men telling lies to women.

4. Men telling lies to men.

In three of the above, people will tell more self-serving lies than kind-hearted ones. In the other one, people will tell the same number of kind-hearted and self-serving. You might be asking which one?

Kind-hearted lies get exchanged between two women more. If men are involved, either as liars or targets, the self-serving lies will always prevail. There were always two to eight times more self-serving lies than kind-hearted lies.

Lying and Age

In the above study, the community people didn't tell as many lies as the college students. This means that older adults won't tell as many lies, right? Well, not really; the community people were different in other aspects as well. There was 81 percent that was employed, and 34 percent just had a high school education.

In a completely different study, adults were asked how many lies they had told in the past 24 hours. The results showed that the older they were, the number of lies told was a lot less. The main difference was that they didn't say how many opportunities they had to tell a lie.

This isn't written in stone, but it might be that the older we get, the less we lie.

Forms of Lying

If you started researching ways to know if someone is lying, you would find many different articles that will give you lists that might include averting eye contact, changes in their voice, fidgeting, and nervousness. If you work, you were interviewed for the job, and these happen a lot. These are all normal reactions to any stressful event.

Spotting a lie is hard to do. Everyone will exhibit different mannerisms when lying rather than a set pattern that is constant for everybody. If someone were to lie during an interview, it might be likely that the majority of what they are saying is true. It's hard to get through all that information to figure out what parts were deceitful while conducting the interview.

It is also hard to lie. A skilled and knowledgeable person knows ways to see and expose lies by using a very detailed inquiry. You can ask the same question in different ways to get more information that will be more accurate. You could consistently rephrase the question until you get all the clarification that you want. If a person is lying, constantly pushing the conversation might lead to new choices; they will have to either escalate their lie or claim that they don't understand and finally tell you the truth. If they do decide to escalate their lie, indicators of lying will become more obvious.

No one can deny that lying is bad. The thing is that most people are completely clueless about to large the problem is. Lying may be an unconscious and destructive habit. Let's look at different lies and see if you recognize any of them.

Understanding the different types of lies could help recognize the problems that a liar may go through, whether they are friends or foes. Knowing the types of lies to look out for might help you when trying to detect a lie:

- Lying for Exaggeration

Exaggerating will enhance the truth when you add a lie to it. A person who exaggerates will mix truths with untruths to make them look more impressive to others. These people could successfully weave truths and lies together to create confusion even to the person who is doing the lying. With time, the liar will start to believe their exaggeration.

Some people think that exaggerating will help them. If you believe that you aren't good at something, you might choose to lie about something to make you sound better. These are very tragic people because they don't feel good about themselves, and they feel like they have to make up stories to make themselves look good around other people.

- Compulsive Lying

This is caused by the person needing attention. This person has very low self-esteem. A person who is a compulsive liar will find it hard to stop lying. They tell their lies even if tell the truth would have been easier and better. Many people believe that each word of what they say is the truth. They live in their little world that is completely different from reality. It isn't ridiculous. It is a tragedy.

- Bold-Faced Lies

This is a type of lie that tells other people something that everybody knows is a lie. It is very simple. It might be cute for small children to tell a lie about not having any cookies before dinner, even if they have chocolate all over their faces.

As we get older, we like to try to be this clever when covering our lies. Some people don't ever grow up and continue to lie even if others know that they tell nothing but lies. When we hear a bald-faced lie, we feel resentful that they think so little about our time and intelligence.

Some might say they hate lying even when they know everybody around them know that they are lying. They might even feel a bit dumb. The people who are being lied to might feel the same way.

- White Lies

This lie is considered the least serious of them all. People claim they tell white lies just to be courteous or polite. It might be just making up an excuse for not attending a party or not showing appreciation for a gift you don't want. Consistently telling white lies could cause conflict because, after some time, they could cause problems with others since they begin to realize the insincerity. This is what causes people who tell white lies to lose credibility.

Saying that you have something to do when you don't know so that you don't have to let them know that you don't want to go out with them can hurt as much as a straight line. Saying that you are fine even when you feel down or sad could hurt you more than the other person. When you tell this little white lie, you disrespect the person who asked that simple question to help build the relationship. It will put up roadblocks when trying to build a deeper relationship.

- Fabrication

This is telling other people things that you aren't even sure they are true. These are very hurtful since they could lead to rumors being started that might damage another person's reputation. Once you decide to begin a rumor about somebody, it isn't just a lie, but you are stealing their reputation. Some people love spreading rumors.

They like telling lies about people you don't like. It works most of the time. You are deliberately inventing false stories.

- Deception

People who like to deceive create impressions that cause others to get misled by creating false impressions or not telling all the facts. You might not like others to think you are smart, so you joke about being smart to try to make them think that you aren't smart. This might work some of the time, and it might not even feel like you are lying. You think you are just pretending to be something that you aren't. Being deceptive is hurtful. It is very subtle but deadly at the same time. It was like when you were a child, and you exaggerated about everything you can do even when you know you can't. You make yourself look more experienced, successful, greater, and better.

- Broken Promises

This is failing to keep a commitment or promise. It can create much damage when a person makes promised that they never had any intention of keeping. Saying you will do something when you know you aren't going to be able to could cause many problems.

What many people don't realize is that lying and breaking a promise can cause double damage. It can cause hurt feelings that never had to happen. Breaking promises can hurt other people's hope. They get excited because you said you could do it just to have their hopes destroyed when you don't. These broken promises could easily lead to lives getting broken.

Here are some more types of lies:

- Restructuring: These distort the context. People will say things sarcastically. They might change the characters or the scene.

- Minimization: They reduce the effects of a mistake, judgment call, or fault.

- Error: This one only a lie by mistake. The person who says these things don't realize that they are lying.

- Denial: These people outright refuse to acknowledge what is true. The extent of their denial could be very large. They might lie just to you one time, or they might just be lying to themselves.

- Omission: They will leave out relevant information. This isn't as risky and a lot easier. They aren't forced to make this up. It's passive deception, and there isn't as much guilt involved.

Non-verbal Signals

By now, you might be wondering how you can tell if a person is lying. This could get complicated. Many people have instincts for detecting a lie, and these are quite strong, but our minds could fail us at times.

There are some signs you could look for when trying to spot a lie. The author of *The Body Language of Liars*, Dr. Lillian Glass, stated that when trying to see if someone is lying to you, you have to know the way this person normally acts. Like pointing while talking or oversharing, certain habits might be just part of that person's character.

Remember that these signs are only indicators of being dishonest and nowhere near positive proof. Some people are such perfect liars that they could get away with not showing any signs at all.

Keep all that in mind while looking at some signs that someone might be lying to you:

- Sweating or Dryness

Changes to a person's autonomic nervous system could trigger a person who is telling a lie to begin sweating in the T-zone on the face. This is the forehead, chin, mouth, and upper lip. They could also turn dry around their mouth and eyes. They might even start to swallow hard, lick or bite their lips, blink excessively, or squint.

- Changing Their Head Position

If you see someone quickly moving their head while asking them questions, they might be lying to you. Their head might also jerk backward, tilt to one side, or bow down. This happens right before they are expected to respond to your question.

- Complexion

Have you ever been talking to somebody and they turn ghostly white? This is another sign that they aren't telling you the truth. This show the blood has rushed out of their face.

- Breathing Changes

If a person is lying, they might begin to breathe heavily. This is normal. If their breathing begins to change, their shoulders will rise, and their voice will get shallow. They will run out of breath since their blood flow and heart rate has changed. Your body goes through these changes if you begin to feel nervous or tense when you lie.

- Mouth

If a person's lips begin to roll to the point that they begin to disappear, it might mean that they are leaving out important pieces of information. When someone does this, they are holding back emotions or facts.

People that lie will purse their lips if they are asked very sensitive questions. Pursing of the lips might mean that someone doesn't want to be a part of your conversation. This is an automatic reflex. This shows that they are not interested in talking.

- Standing Extremely Still

People will normally fidget if they get nervous, but you should look for people who aren't moving.

This might be a sign of the body's fight mode rather than the flight response, as it gets ready for a confrontation. When you engage in conversations, it is normal to move around in subtle, relaxed, and unconscious movements. If you notice somebody in a rigid, catatonic stance where they aren't moving at all, this is a big warning that something is very wrong.

- Eyes

A person who is lying might either look away or stare during crucial moments. If they move their eyes a lot, it could be a sign that they are trying to figure out what they would like to say next.

Geiselman from UCLA found that liars will look away very fast when they are lying. In a 2015 study performed at the University of Michigan, it was discovered that liars would stare at others more often than people who were telling the truth. Around 70 percent of the people who lied would stare directly at the person they are lying to.

There have been debates about this, but an article published in *Plos One* in 2012 said this concept. They concluded that people would look in a certain direction if they are lying. While it is very easy to read too much into how a person is acting, you can gain a lot from their eyes.

- Touching Their Mouth

A sure sign that a person isn't telling the truth is they will place either their hands on their mouth if they aren't interested in answering a question or facing a problem.

When adults cover their mouths with their hands, they show you that they aren't truthful in what they are saying, and they aren't interested in telling you the truth. They are showing you that they are closing down all lines of communication.

- Being Fidgety

Some other signs of deception might include a person who is shuffling their feet, moving their head from side to side, or rocking back and forth on their feet or in their seat. This is created by fluctuations in our autonomic nervous system that regulates functions throughout our bodies and could also create an effect. If someone is shy, these fluctuations could cause a person to feel itchy or tingly, causing them to fidget even more.

R. Edward Geiselman, a professor at UCLA, conducted some research and found a very similar conclusion. He found that people will display certain grooming behaviors like playing with their hair if they aren't truthful.

- Covering Vulnerable Body Parts

This could include parts such as the chest, head, throat, or abdomen. Go to any courtroom and just watch people. You will be able to spot when a witness is lying or if a testimony hits a nerve with the defendant if their hand goes to their throat.

- Hands

Liars like using gestures after they have spoken instead of before or during the conversation, state Traci Brown, an FBI consultant. Their minds are busy doing many different things like making up their story, seeing if people believe them, and adding in more details. Common gestures that regularly happen just before speaking usually happen after they talk.

The University of Michigan performed a study in 2015 that studied 120 video clips of relevant court cases to understand how people act when they are lying versus when they are telling the truth. This study showed that people who lie would gesture using both hands. People who are telling the truth usually use just one hand. People used both hands around 40 percent of the time compared to 25 percent of the people who are telling the truth.

If a person is lying, they will normally turn their palms away from their speaking person. This is an unconscious signal to you that they are withholding emotions or information. They might even put them under a table or in their pockets.

- Shuffling Their Feet

This is their body taking over. When a person starts to shuffle their feet, this is showing you that they are nervous and uncomfortable. It shows you that they want to walk away from the conversation. This is a great way to spot liars. What their feet and they will tell you a lot.

- The Point

If a person gets hostile or defensive, they are trying to turn things around on you. If they get confronted about a lie, they might begin using aggressive gestures like pointing.

- Staring But Not Blinking

If a person is lying, it is common for them to break eye contact, but some liars will go the extra mile to keep eye contact to manipulate and control you. If someone is telling you the truth, they might occasionally shift their eye and might look away now, and then, Liars will use a steady gaze to control and intimidate. Watch out for rapid blinking, too.

Verbal Signals

Here are some changes to a person's voice when they are lying:

- Hard Time Speaking

If you have watched a suspect gets interrogated and you know they are guilty, you will see it get hard for them to talk. This will happen because their nervous system lowers the flow of saliva in stressful times, causing the mucous membranes of the mouth to become dry. If they purse or bite their lips, these are also signs that they are lying.

- Voice if High-pitched

If someone is nervous, their vocal cords might tighten up, causing their voice to sound high-pitched. Their voice might also creak. They might clear their throat, meaning they are trying to cope with how uncomfortable their throat feels. It could also signal a lie.

- Giving Lots of Information

If someone is constantly talking and giving you all sorts of information and this information isn't anything that you haven't even asked for, and they seem to be providing a lot of little details, this is a good indicator lying. Liars will talk more because they hope that talking a lot and being open will make people believe them.

- Changes in Volume

If a person is telling a lie, they might raise their voice. Their voice might get louder because they are feeling defensive.

- Repeating Specific Words or Phrases

This happens because they are trying to convince themselves and you of something. They are trying to prove the lie to themselves. They might repeat, "I didn't... I didn't..." constantly.

This repetition is a way to buy them some time while they try to gather their thoughts.

- They Use Certain Phrases

If someone likes using phrases like: "let me tell you the truth," "honestly," or "I would like to be honest with you." These are all signs that they might be trying extremely hard or little to convince you that they are honest.

- Slip-Ups

Many people aren't born liars. Most of the time, we will let the truth slip out. Take notice if someone says things like: "I got fired – no, I meant I quit" or "I had dinner with Frank – no, I meant I had to work late." You might just have a liar in your presence.

- They Use Certain Words

If a person frequently uses words such as: "um," "like," or "uh," they are using what is called vocal fill, and these are all deception indicators. People will use these fillers to figure out what they need to say next.

Conclusion

Thank you for making it through to the end of *How to Analyze People with Psychology*. Let's hope it was informative and able to provide you with all of the tools you need to achieve your goals, whatever they may be.

Body language can fill you in on the hidden bits of information that people don't want you to know. It can let you know if a person is interested in what you have to say or if you are simply wasting your breath. You may discover a person that you thought didn't like you, actually does. You never know what you will learn through body language, which makes it such a powerful tool. Use the ability to read people wisely, however. Some people are simply fidgety, so you can't assume that everybody who picks their nails is lying. Look at the big picture and make sure you know the person before you jumped to any conclusions based solely on their body language.

Finally, if you found this book useful in any way, a review on Amazon is always appreciated!

CPSIA information can be obtained
at www.ICGtesting.com
Printed in the USA
BVHW051532050821
613735BV00011B/1022